MASTER YOUR EMOTIONS

Discover How to end Anxiety, Overcome Negativity, Stop Overthinking and Control your Thoughts to Definitely Change your Life

Nills Scot

© Written By Nills Scot

© Copyright 2019 by - All rights reserved

Respective authors own all copyrights not held by the publisher.

The information herein is offered for informational purposes solely, and is universal as so. The presentation of the information is without contract or any type of guarantee assurance.

The trademarks that are used are without any consent, and the publication of the trademark is without permission or backing by the trademark owner. All trademarks and brands within this book are for clarifying purposes only and are the owned by the owners themselves, not affiliated with this document.

Disclaimer and Terms of Use: The Author and Publisher has strived to be as accurate and complete as possible in the creation of this book, notwithstanding the fact that he does not warrant or represent at any time that the contents within are accurate due to the rapidly changing nature of the Internet. While all attempts have been made to verify information provided in this publication, the Author and Publisher assumes no responsibility for errors, omissions, or contrary interpretation of the subject matter herein.

Any perceived slights of specific persons, peoples, or organizations are unintentional. In practical advice books, like anything else in life, there are no guarantees of results. Readers are cautioned to rely on their own judgment about their individual circumstances and act accordingly.

This book is not intended for use as a source of legal, medical, business, accounting or financial advice. All readers are advised to seek services of competent professionals in the legal, medical, business, accounting, and finance fields.

Table of Contents

Introduction

The more we try to block our emotions, the more they will come hunting us. The more we avoid an emotion, the bigger and the more powerful it gets, until the energy becomes too much that it finds its way out of our system, often in the form of an illness, or some kind of unpleasant body manifestation.

My favorite definition of Emotion is one from Michael Sky, firewalking instructor, breathwork teacher, and certified Energy breath and polarity therapist. He defines emotions as: energy-in-motion: Emotional energy that exists as a constant flowing presence in our lives. He refers to Human Feelings as subtle currents, part liquid, part electric that arise as vital energy moving within, around, and between us, animating spirits, coloring thoughts, influencing dreams, heartening relationships, and providing the raw material for our bodies and creative efforts. What a beautiful way to describe what we know as feelings!

All of our emotions manifest as moving (arising, vibrating, gathering, flowing, expanding, boiling) energy. When we have a feeling of any kind we experience a tangible movement of vital energy in our body. The energy moving through us comprises the feeling: such energy moving is emotion.

When we grow up we are not taught how to deal with emotions, how to acknowledge them and cope with them in a beneficial way. How many times do we have an open discussion about emotions and feelings with our family? It is very rare, which is in part why emotion often troubles and torments us.

Over time people develop strategies for feeling less, since emotion seems to afflict us, we find ways to suppress our emotional experience. We learn to deaden out feelings, to turn off sensation, to numb out. We strive to prevail, unaffected by life's changes. Nothing more unhealthy an unnatural than doing that!

Society often tells us that emotional expression belongs to the world of children, while maturing means getting one's emotions under control. In today's society emotional people are often looked as weak; we favor those who remain firm and clearheaded during the worst times. We specially despise the messiness of emotional display. It is often wrongly believed that spiritual advancement requires the taming of one's feelings. We try to "avoid pain" by acting without feeling, doing things rationally and logically, and by doing so, we are only denying our human nature.

Ultimately some people find their own way with emotion, some manage to completely suppress their feelings and keep their emotional energy unexpressed in order to be socially acceptable. That so many people do so well at suppressing their emotions constitutes a singular failure in human development and a root cause of many problems of society nowadays, especially stress which converts into illnesses of different kinds.

Emotion plays an essential role in our lives, for better and for worse that emotional energy subsists as a vital force in the human organism and as an interconnection between body, mind, spirit, and environment.

So what do we do with emotions?

Learning to flow with ones feelings opens the way to physical health, mental clarity, greater success in relationships, and more effective creativity.

How do we flow with our feelings?
One way of flowing with our feelings is to actively accept or acknowledge our emotions, as opposed to blocking them. In other words keeping our emotional energies in perpetual motion and finally, direct all those energies to good creative use. The ultimate goal is to form an appreciation for the beauty and power of all sorts of human emotions, learn to live with them and use them to our advantage. We can try in vain to stop feeling stressed, angry, and sad, etc. or we can tap in to the strong energies of those feelings and channel them toward effective response.

Any perceived threat might cause the arousal of fear-energy. Even when the threat is unreal (product of our mind or imagination) Ignoring such "unreal" fears rarely works because the fear-energy they generate is all too real and will find resolution- one way or another. It will find its way out of our system eventually and often in an unpleasant or uncomfortable way.

Life changes constantly, and often those changes create situations that confront and challenge us. Those changes that we perceive as threatening to the body, family, home, religion, country, and planet will trigger feelings of fear, anxiety and tension, etc. Such feelings arise as a force for effective response, they are the creative power needed to successfully deal with whatever happens.

Just as fear-energy arises in response to specific perceptions, likewise does the full range of human emotion. Each of us perceives life's changes in different ways according to our education, stage in life an experiences, each of us has a unique perception of life, or what Miguel Ruiz refers to as " the dream" in his book "The Mastery of Love". We perceive reality and then emotionally respond to our perceptions. Considering our nature as emotional beings, how we deal with the constant flux of emotional energies will largely impact our success and failure in life, our happiness and unhappiness.

What else can we do to deal with emotions?
Other important factor in dealing effectively with emotions is the degree to which we accept life's unfolding, events in our life and flow with them. When what we want in a situation corresponds with what actually happens, then we tend to experience the energy moving within us as a positive emotion, we feel good! The good feeling comes from our acceptance of what happens, including the present movement of energies. We are happy in those moments when we easily accept the movement of life, including the moving of energy of our emotional process. When we accept our immediate perception of reality, then the movement of vital energy comes in a variation of emotions such as: joy, peace, faith, trust, inspiration, devotion.

When we experience the opposite and what actually happens is not what we want or expect, the emotional energy within us is unpleasant, we simply don't feel good an often our response is to resist, avoid, and reject such energy. When we don't accept life's changes and resist to them, we experience a range of negative emotions such as: disappointment, sadness, feeling of failure, anger, resentment, etc. All those emotions are part of our humanness as well and they provide the raw material to respond effectively if we channel them properly.

Our system is perfectly designed to cry, crying is a cleanser, it helps us wash away emotions that need to leave our body, and we must let them come out. Perhaps when we were younger we were told not to cry many times, it is often seen as a sign of weakness, we all have heard... " Men don't cry" or big girls don't cry" How wrong those statements are! Young, old, women or men, we were designed to cry and with the right to cry.

We have the right to feel angry, sad, joyful, anxious, nervous, excited, etc, etc... we have the right to be drama queens once in a while. What is not valid is to get stuck in the drama and affect others around us or want other to join us in our sadness or anger, or hurt others with the excuse that we are only expressing our emotions. It is important to acknowledge emotions and to have the awareness to channel and use them in our best interest, use its power in a positive way.

The more I read and try to understand life and its purpose; I have come to conclude that the only purpose of our existence is to live life to the fullest. Live the glory and the pain, with intensity, with passion, with sentiment, because we were designed to feel and to express our feelings. Being honest and faithful with ourselves and our feelings will take us to fulfillment.

Give yourself the right to experience your humanness to the fullest. Live the joy and the pain with passion, travel to your drama place, or anger place as often as you need, but don't stay there permanently and don't carry other people with you either.

The more we accept ourselves, other people, circumstances and events, the more positively enjoyable and supportive our emotional energies become.

What are emotions?

Emotions, often called feelings, include experiences such as love, hate, anger, trust, joy, panic, fear, and grief. Emotions are related to, but different from, mood. Emotions are specific reactions to a particular event that are usually of fairly short duration. Mood is a more general feeling such as happiness, sadness, frustration, contentment, or anxiety that lasts for a longer time.

Although everyone experiences emotions, scientists do not all agree on what emotions are or how they should be measured or studied. Emotions are complex and have both physical and mental components. Generally researchers agree that emotions have the following parts: subjective feelings, physiological (body) responses, and expressive behavior.

The component of emotions that scientists call subjective feelings refers to the way each individual person experiences feelings, and this component is the most difficult to describe or measure. Subjective feelings cannot be observed; instead, the person experiencing the emotion must describe it to others, and each person's description and interpretation of a feeling may be slightly different. For example, two people falling in love will not experience or describe their feeling in exactly the same ways.

Physiological responses are the easiest part of emotion to measure because scientists have developed special tools to measure them. A pounding heart, sweating, blood rushing to the face, or the release of adrenaline * in response to a situation that creates intense emotion can all be measured with scientific accuracy. People have very similar internal responses to the same emotion. For example, regardless of age, race, or gender, when people are under stress, their bodies release adrenaline; this hormone helps prepare the body to either run away or fight, which is called the "fight or flight" reaction. Although the psychological part of emotions may be different for each feeling, several different emotions can produce the same physical reaction.

Expressive behavior is the outward sign that an emotion is being experienced. Outward signs of emotions can include fainting, a flushed face, muscle tensing, facial expressions, tone of voice, rapid breathing, restlessness, or other body language. The outward expression of an emotion gives other people clues to what someone is experiencing and helps to regulate social interactions.

* adrenaline (a-DREN-a-lin), also called epinephrine, (ep-e-NEF-rin), is a hormone, or chemical messenger, that is released In response to fear, anger, panic, and other emotions. It readies the body to respond to threat by increasing heart rate, breath-Ing rate, and blood flow to the arms and legs. These and other effects prepare the body to run away or fight.

Why Do We Have Emotions?

Emotions appear to serve several physical and psychological purposes. Some scientists believe that emotions are one of the fundamental traits associated with being human. Emotions color people's lives and give them depth and differentiation. For many people, strong emotions are linked to creativity and expression. Great art, music, and literature deal on a fundamental level with arousing emotions and creating an emotional connection between the artist and the public. Some scientists also believe that emotions serve as motivation to behave in specific ways.

The French neurologist Guillaume Duchenne (1806-1875) studied the body's neuromuscular system. In this experiment (c. 1855), he used an electrical stimulation device to activate the involuntary facial muscles involved in smiling and laughter.

Physiologically, emotions aid in survival. For example, sudden fear often causes a person to freeze like a deer caught by a car's headlights. Because animals usually attack in response to motion, at its simplest level, fear reduces the chances of attack. When Mandy froze in response to a car racing by her, this was an example of a physical response to an emotion that improved her chances of survival.

Emotions also help people monitor their social behavior and regulate their interactions with others. Every person unconsciously learns to "read" the outward expressions of other people and apply past experience to determine what these outward signs indicate about what the other person is feeling. If a person sees a man approaching who is walking very aggressively, holding his body stiffly and frowning, the person might correctly assume that the man is angry. Using this information, the person can decide whether to leave or to stay or what tone of voice and body language to use when approaching the man.

Some outward expressions of emotions (body language) mean different things in different cultures. For example, if a young person avoids looking directly at a person in authority, it is taken as a sign of respect in some cultures. In other cultures, this expression suggests guilt or a lack of trustworthiness.

Understanding Your Emotions

Everything you need to know about why you feel the way you do.

Our emotions are crucial to your ability to adapt to the challenges of your daily life. When you feel good, you're able to shrug off even the most burdensome of tasks, but when you're miserable, you view even an enjoyable activity with a sense of gloom and doom. Emotions also affect our relationships with others. If a friend tells you a tragic story and you react by snickering instead of looking sad or concerned, you'll seem rude and insensitive. On the other hand, if you frown when you should smile at your friend's jokes, you'll cause offense for different reasons.

Flying off the handle to a minor annoyance can make you seem hyper or even unbalanced. Conversely, if you react with undue glee to a relatively minor piece of good news, people will also question your maturity and stability.   Babies are allowed to shriek with pleasure or howl with rage but as adults, we're expected to rein in the outward show of our feelings.

If you need more convincing proof about the role of emotions in our ability to succeed or fail in facing life's challenges, think about some of the famous people whose careers have been undone by the improper show of their feelings. In the primary run up to the 2004 presidential election, Howard Dean's candidacy ended virtually overnight after his "YAAAAHHH" moment became an overnight Internet sensation. Edmund Muskie, in the 1972 primary season, committed a similar political gaffe in which he shed tears after winning the New Hampshire primary (though he claimed they were snowflakes shimmering in the morning light). Ironically, tears are all the rage in the post-2000 political world. Hillary Clinton wasn't considered sympathetic enough until her eyes misted over while answering a voter's question (again in New Hampshire!), but many pundits used this against her to question her sincerity. Then there's the sentimental carryings-one of House Republican leader John Boehner, whose tear ducts seem on constant overdrive.

These examples show not only that the outward display of inner feelings influences how we're regarded by others, but also that these emotional displays are heavily dependent on cultural norms. To be regarded as a well-adapted member of society we need to adhere to those norms or risk condemnation or ridicule. Psychologist Paul Ekman showed that there are six basic emotions that people of all cultures experience and recognize (happiness, sadness, surprise, anger, fear, and disgust). How and when we express these emotions differs radically by the norms of each of our cultures, the so-called display rules.

Our emotions affect not only the way others treat us, but our inner sense of well-being. We tend to believe that whether we are experiencing positive or negative emotions reflects forces outside our control, blaming everything from our genes to the weather. However, what many people do not realize is that emotions aren't strictly controlled by your body's physiology the way that reflexes are. You're not stuck for life with the emotional equipment programmed into your DNA.

To understand the way that you can control your emotions, we first have to take a slight detour through the early history of psychology. Views about what emotions are, and what causes them, have changed radically in the last 100 or so years. To take this journey, who better to start with than William James, the founder of American psychology? According to James, and the closely related views of physiologist Carl Lange, your emotions are completely governed by your body's responses. In fact, they are the emotions. Imagine you're being pursued by a bear. If you're like most of us, fear and panic will take over your entire being, causing your heart to race, your palms to get sweaty, and your stomach to turn somersaults. James and Lange equated these responses of your autonomic nervous system with the actual emotion of fear. According to their theory (known to intro psych students as the infamous "James-Lange Theory"), your bodily reaction doesn't follow the emotion, it is the emotion. As James said, "Common sense says we lose our fortune, are sorry and weep; we meet a bear, are frightened and run; we are insulted by a rival, are angry and strike, afraid because we tremble... the more rational statement is that we feel sorry because we cry, angry because we strike, afraid because we tremble" (Ellsworth, 1994, p. 222). Quite literally, when James and Lange talked about a "visceral" (or gut) emotional reaction, they meant it.

Many people found the James-Lange theory hard to accept. Common sense seems to work out just fine, despite James' assertion. Apart from the theory just "feeling" wrong (so to speak), it also failed to meet the test of scientific acceptability and was therefore eventually dropped as an explanation.

One very similar theory that appeared soon after the James-Lange foray into the field was that proposed by physiologist Walter Cannon; a view that is now known as the "Cannon-Bard" theory (reflecting his collaboration with a doctoral student named Philip Bard). This theory proposes that our emotions are regulated by the reaction of a small structure in the brain known as the thalamus. It's the thalamus that would sense, for example, the onrushing bear. This sensation simultaneously causes the visceral reactions in the body and the subjective experience in the brain. The Cannon-Bard theory eventually became discredited too because it did not withstand experimental scrutiny. The thalamus may be involved in some emotional regulation, but it's not the brain's hot spot for our feelings. Instead, the amygdala seems to be the culprit when it comes to such emotions as fear, rage, and jealousy.

The idea that our emotions may be controllable started to emerge in the theory developed by Stanley Schachter and Jerome Singer in the early 1960s. In their now classic psychology experiment, they led college students to believe that they were receiving a trial dose of a vitamin. In fact, the experimenters injected the students with epinephrine. The students then watched a "confederate" (another student acting out experimental instructions) who became either angry or euphoric while completing a set of questionnaires. The students exposed to the angry confederate reported that they felt angry; those exposed to the euphoric confederate said they felt happy. The results showed that the combination of arousal (caused by epinephrine) and context (the confederate's behavior) influenced the emotional state of the experimental subject.

To translate, the Schachter-Singer study implies that your emotions are influenced by what's going on in the people around you and which emotions they're expressing. Another term for this is "emotional contagion." If you've ever felt moved to cry at the wedding of people you don't know very well because everyone around you is weeping into their hankies, you know how these feelings can catch on. (Why we cry at weddings is another story.)

Your emotions don't have to fall prey to those being expressed by the people around you, though. The cognitive revolution in emotion theory, led by University of Pennsylvania psychiatrist Aaron Beck, showed that our thoughts alone can produce our emotions. Beck's studies of depressed individuals led him to the discovery that dysfunctional attitudes and negatively-framed automatic thoughts are at the root of people's feelings of sadness. A dysfunctional attitude is a way of viewing the world that focuses on the negative and unrealistic aspects of your experiences. A negatively-framed automatic thought is an unconscious belief that focuses on your weaknesses rather than your strengths. Together, dysfunctional attitudes and automatic thoughts create the "negative triad" consisting of a negative view of yourself, your world, and your future. The extensive research based on Beck's theory has led to acceptance of his cognitive-behavioral method of therapy as the premier treatment of depression.

Even if you're not clinically depressed, you can borrow a page from Beck's playbook to understand your emotions. For instance, sadness is caused by the belief that you've lost or will lose something important to you, anger is caused by the belief that someone has taken something away from you, and anxiety is based on the belief that something bad will happen to you. Unrealistically distorting your experiences produces these thoughts which then lead to your negative emotions.

Rational-emotive psychologist Albert Ellis takes another approach to cognitive theory, accounting more broadly for our tendencies to let our thoughts produce our own self-produced misery. Ellis believed that through "musturbation" we allow our emotions to be dominated by the "must's": "I must be successful," "I must be loved," "I must have what I want." Ellis talked about the "A-B-C" model of emotion:

A: Activating event (a friend turns you down for dinner)

+B: Belief (no one likes me)

=C: Consequence (sad mood, feelings of rejection)

To change the consequence (i.e. your emotion), you need to change your beliefs. To change your beliefs you need to examine them. In this example, you can change the belief that "no one likes me" by looking at the evidence for this belief. Why do you think that no one likes you? Does one person's turning you down mean that no one likes you? Does this mean that no one will ever like you? Does it mean that you must have everyone like you? (This is "musturbation.")

It's through challenging your thoughts and beliefs about yourself that you can change your emotional reactions. Once you start to pick apart the illogical basis for your emotions you can free yourself from being dominated by the maladaptive emotions of rage, jealousy, rejection, and dejection and instead boost your adaptive emotions of happiness, contentment, and joy.

Now that you've given your thoughts this readjustment, you've got one more job to do. According to the "facial feedback hypothesis" of emotion, the expression on your face can influence your emotional state. When you activate the muscles that control your facial expressions, you actually trigger internal changes that lead to the corresponding mood. If you frown, you'll feel mad. If you turn the corners of your mouth down, you'll feel sad. And if you turn the corners of your mouth up in a smile you'll feel good. As the song says, to "make gray skies clear up," just "put on a happy face!"

With this emotional repair kit, you'll be able to make more than the gray skies clear up. You don't have to be held hostage by your gut, your thalamus, or even your amygdala. Focus on the thoughts that precede your emotions and you'll find that you can control your mood. And remember to smile!

What is Ego?

According to Sigmund Freud, the ego is the part of personality that mediates the demands of the id, the superego, and reality. Freud described the id as the most basic part of personality that urges people to fulfill their most primal needs. The superego, on the other hand, is the moralistic part of personality that forms later in childhood as a result of upbringing and social influences. It is the ego's job to strike a balance between these two often competing for forces and to make sure that fulfilling the needs of the id and superego conform to the demands of reality.

A Closer Look at the Ego

The ego prevents us from acting on our basic urges (created by the id) but also works to achieve a balance with our moral and idealistic standards (created by the superego). While the ego operates in both the preconscious and conscious, its strong ties to the id mean that it also operates in the unconscious.

The ego operates based on the reality principle, which works to satisfy the id's desires in a manner that is realistic and socially appropriate. For example, if a person cuts you off in traffic, the ego prevents you from chasing down the car and physically attacking the offending driver. The ego allows us to see that this response would be socially unacceptable, but it also allows us to know that there are other more appropriate means of venting our frustration.

A Healthy Ego - The Key to Mastering Life

Understanding the role of the ego in how we live our lives is essential to understanding the mystery of life.

Usually when people describe themselves they are referring to the ego self or the personality, the finite side of the whole package we call me. We speak about our likes, dislikes, what we do to fill up our days. We speak of others regarding the actions they take in their lives.

Anything that refers to an action or an outer expression is filtered through the ego. This is neither good nor bad; it is just a function of the human mind. Most of us have a habit of automatically judging the goodness or badness of a statement based on how much risk it perpetuates on our own ego. It is part of our safety process.

Until we have accumulated a good understanding of how the ego tarnishes our perception of the world, we cannot really begin to develop a strong mind management process that will allow us to escape from the trappings of the ego mind.

In this article, I am going to do my best to explain to you the difference between living in the ego and living with your ego.

If you analyze any advertising material, you will quickly discover that it is speaking to your ego. It wants you to be beautiful, healthy, wealthy and pain-free. The advertising needs you to give up your personal power and buy into their beliefs. Because so many of us feel less than absolutely wonderful, we buy into their marketing ploys allowing ourselves to feel better, much better.

But is the change in our feeling temporary or is it permanent?

We learned to feed our mind this way through our childhood development. We wanted to please Mom and Dad so that we got our fix of feeling good and loved. When we didn't do the required activity to get our dose of feeling good, we received something that caused us to feel lack. Since we don't like the feeling of going without, our mind devises methods for helping us feel satisfied (healthy or otherwise).

As we go through our lives, depending on how well we were fed with love, trust and confidence as a child, we constantly search for food for our egos so we can believe we feel good. Sometimes, in extreme cases, this establishes habits that are extremely destructive such as alcoholism, drug use, sexual inappropriateness and abuse and control over others.

When we live our lives in any of these manners, even if it is temporary, we are living in the ego.

Living in the ego is not a bad thing. It is limiting to the full life expression though. If we are so consumed with trying to feel good, we have little time for being or doing well. It is like the lion out on the African Savannahs who is constantly in search of the next morsel of food. There just is little or no time for living beyond need.

If we are going to find any true satisfaction in this life, we need to get past the trappings of the ego and learn to live with the ego in our true selves.

There is a huge difference between the two mental positions. We have already demonstrated some activities that are ego based, so what does it look like or feel like to live in truth?

There are two really important aspects of our mind. They are the personality (ego mind) and the character (the true self or higher mind).

The personality is temporary. It lives in the moment and for the moment. Once its purpose is fulfilled, it moves onto another aspect of the personality to suit the needs of the next moment. One moment you are elated from the praise you received for doing something well, then the next moment you are angry because someone slighted you. That is personality.

The character is infinite. It is an aspect of the soul, the only permanent part of you. When you commit an act based on the need of the act rather than your own aggrandizement or glory, you are in character. This is not a case of self deprecation. It is a case of doing what is right for that situation.

As we mature in life, we feel the unrest and dissatisfaction of living in the ego. The highs and lows of constantly searching for food for our vanity wears thin, we crave for something more permanent and fulfilling. This is the higher mind calling, trying to bring you out of the cloud of ego. It is called a calling of purpose.

As we move more deeply into the Aquarian Age, the call for this transition is speaking louder. The Universe needs us to mature and move into a higher form of activity that is beyond survival mode. It requires moving into the higher self.

How do we make this transition?

When we strongly feel the desire to live life more deeply, we feel the unrest that sits in our ego mind. As we become ready, we start using the energy of this feeling of unrest to empower us to embrace our higher journey. It helps us to maneuver past the fears and controls of the ego mind.

Just becoming aware of this feeling is all that is required to begin the transition. The next step is to become very aware of how we allow the ego to mold the goings-on in our lives.

Once we can see the ego at work, it is much easier to take a more conscious approach to life. We begin questioning the choices we have made in the past. We start consciously choosing different outcomes. Eventually this process causes the habitual outcomes to change just through conscious choice and repetition.

A second and very important matter in the process of transitioning from ego living to healthy living is the acceptance of yourself and your capabilities. It sounds odd and even ego based to say this but we need to accept that we are good and great. The difference being that we accept ourselves internally rather than needing to have others validate us from the outside.

In western society, we have made it taboo to cheer ourselves on. We have made it acceptable only to chastise ourselves for our imperfections. How often do we see and hear people who have done really well who upon receiving compliments, minimize them by focusing on their imperfections.

We all need to do this, no matter how old we are. We need to accept the fact that we are blessed with some wonderful skills and we need to cheer ourselves on when we apply them. When we do less than perfect, we need to accept that we did our best, give ourselves space to be human and know that we will learn how to do better by trying again. This is called loving ourselves! Being our own best friend.

When we are able to see ourselves in truth, without letting the ego run the show, we are in our true self, our character. The more often we can do this and recognize ourselves as we do, the more integrated we become with ourselves. As we learn to accept ourselves in our own unique expression of greatness, the power of the ego will settle down to its appropriate level.

It does not matter what other people think of us. If we can come to terms with ourselves, if we can learn to realize and accept when we are acting in ego and when we can love ourselves just for being the wonderful person we were created as, then we are on the path to having a healthy ego and a healthy life.

We do not need to eliminate the ego or constantly undermine the wealth we offer to the world in order to be acceptable to society and ourselves. In order to offer best value to all life, we need to be all we are. Living in full self with purpose is living with a healthy ego.

I urge you as you ponder your thoughts about this section of the eBook to take some time for introspection. What more can you do to express the amazing person you were born as? What more can you do to live a better, healthier and more fulfilling life? What do you need to do so that your ego can feel safe so it can let you have the freedom that is your birth right?

The Ego at Work - Some Solutions

The ego is a fact of life. People identify with their thoughts, beliefs and perceptions and will staunchly defend their resulting identifications. The core of the ego is attachment, resistance and separation. In the context of organisation development, we have to deal with the ego as it is. The solution to the ego at the organisational level, is facing up to it and developing the organisation in a way that recognises the ego and its downsides. A similar approach works at an individual level. This may be simple, but is far from easy. There is no soft option of being aware of others' egos - there is only one ego (that displays itself in different ways) so if we are serious about addressing the implications of the ego at work, we need to look at the ego patterns within ourselves. They are there, the only issue is whether we have faced up to those patterns. Indeed, a fast track approach is to operate from the belief that perception is projection, that what we perceive in others reflects to some extent the patterns within ourselves. (This is not something that can be "proven", rather it is a helpful operating belief). As Byron Katie says: "everyone is a mirror image of yourself, your own thinking coming back at you."

There are three keys to addressing the ego at work: awareness, acceptance and depersonalisation.

Awareness

The more we are aware - moment by moment- of the ego and its programmes, the more we can begin to transcend its behaviour patterns. The challenge here is that intellectual awareness is not sufficient, only mindfulness moment by moment is sufficiently powerful to overcome the deep set patterns of defending the ego's identifications.

It helps to be aware that the ego will always look to create a sense of separation, between itself and the rest of the world, and also between other things in the world. So the ego will identify itself as the victim of "unfairness", "the economy", and others' behaviours, thereby placing itself as being at effect of circumstances. It will even blame the behaviours of the person it considers itself to be on circumstances, if those behaviours are considered undesirable. Yet, the ego is happy to claim to be at cause when it wants to claim its successes, its "amazing results", its positive behaviours. So the ego projects the cause of what is undesirable outside itself, and claims the cause of what is desirable as itself. It is willing to alternate between self-pity and pride, whichever bolsters its sense of separation.

The sense of separation is also maintained by comparison. Most people would associate a sense of being "better" as egotistical. But the ego can also juice subconscious satisfaction from being "poorer", "disadvantaged", or the loser. The ego can maintain its sense of self by being angry, being afraid, or even though hatred. It can use moral superiority, a sense of being elite, or even "not being part of the elite". Negative emotions tend to make us pay attention to negative aspects of our situation, which then makes us perceive even more negativity. A lack of gratitude for the positive things we have means we are less likely to hold on to them.

The ego will also maintain the sense of separation, by regarding its beliefs, memories, thoughts and experiences, as not just "mine", but "me". The ego's purpose is to preserve its idea of "me", therefore it will resist anything that challenges that sense of self. So if it is identified with (and thereby attached to) a particular strategy, it will resist changing strategy until the evidence is overwhelming that this needs to happen. By then, the business or career may have suffered immense damage.

In order to hold on to the sense of the familiar, the ego will hold on to "clutter". This may be physical clutter (often based on an unconscious fear of lack). Or often it is the clutter of holding onto patterns, even though they don't work, because they seem familiar and because we are afraid of what stillness and silence would reveal. The ego is reluctant to let go. Yet letting go is at the heart of all growth. Even money only get its power as it is circulated and let go of (e.g through investment or wise spending) rather than hoarded.

There is a positive path in awareness too. This involves the realisation of what is deeply obvious, but often forgotten moment by moment. The awareness in "others" is as subjectively real as the awareness in "me". We are not the centre of the universe. The ego, however, is identified with the content of the awareness of each individual, rather than the impersonal awareness in which thoughts, beliefs, memories etc happen. The more attention is placed on the awareness in others being as real as that in ourselves, the more effective we are at teamwork, influence and customer service.

Acceptance

What we resist, we make stronger. Fighting the ego simply feeds it. We have to be, as Jesus said, "subtle as serpents, innocent [i.e. open-minded] as doves". If we operate from the perspective that perception is projection, then we can understand that what we perceive around us, both "positive" and "negative" reflects some aspect of what is within ourselves. It therefore makes no sense to be "against" what we perceive, rather it makes more sense to focus on how we would prefer things to be, whilst accepting that what is before us now is the starting point for any change. If we resist the starting point - i.e.what is before us right now, we cannot promote effective change. For example, an individual or a nation can defend itself more effectively if they simply acknowledge they are under attack and deal with it, rather than wallowing in denial, anger or self-pity.

Acceptance, therefore, does not mean passivity. Denial tends to result in delay and paralysis, whereas acceptance creates the space for a solution. Our idea of how things "should" be is just a hypothetical idea. The hypothetical is not the real. Rather than wasting energy on how things "should" be, it is more effective to deal with things as they are.

Depersonalisation

As a training consultant, when running sessions on how to give effective feedback, I always emphasised the importance of focusing on behaviours, not identity. People inevitably will defend their sense of self. (So for example, telling your boss "you're a bad manager" is unlikely to help their behaviour, or your career!) I would explore with delegates how best to give feedback in a way that sold the benefits of changing behaviour, rather than criticising the person.

So part of an effective strategy for minimising the impact of the ego, is depersonalising discussion of behaviours. Indeed, this can be just as important for positive behaviours as for negative. Certain attitudes, behaviours, and strategies are more likely to result in success. By depersonalising the process, by focusing on the ingredients of success rather than a mythical separate "me" you can think in terms of attitudes, behaviours and strategies that can be shared with others. Those around you can learn from the approach you used, which means they will be more successful and help you be more successful in turn. It is also important to be aware of the context in which the attitudes, behaviours and strategies worked. They may be less effective (or more) in a different context.

It is wise to value the contribution made through you by the behaviours, attitude and strategies you use. But that is different from using your success to bolster the idea of a self independent and separate from the world around you.

Having a goal that is "bigger than us" e.g making progress on addressing a problem in society, can help manage the ego. However, the ego is more than capable of identifying itself with the larger cause, using the bigger cause to emphasise the difference between itself and others. (This is a root of fanaticism of all types and the attitude that the end justifies the means.) We can practice impersonal devotion, devotion to the universal values of growth and truth, rather than to our particular way of living out those values.

As we become aware of the ego's "tricks" and accept how those tricks operate both within and around us, we can begin to diminish the ego's hold by depersonalising how we think about behaviours. We are then more free and open to explore what really works for us and our colleagues.

What Impacts Your Emotions?

Impact Of Sleep On Your Mood

Getting enough sleep, and the right type of sleep, is vital for our overall health and wellbeing. While you sleep, your body works to support healthy brain functions and maintain your physical health. And for children and young people, sleep is how their bodies and minds grow and develop.

When you do not get enough sleep, you feel tired, you find it hard to concentrate and remember things and you may be grumpy. Lack of sleep can also impair your judgement and impact your physical coordination. So not getting enough sleep affects the way you feel, think, work, learn and get along with other people.

If you are having problems getting to sleep or staying asleep, or if you often feel tired during the day, you may need to work out what's happening. But the good news is most sleeping problems are easily fixed.

Sleep and moods

Think about how one bad night's sleep, or not enough sleep, makes you feel the next day. For many of us, we're grumpy and irritable, we find it difficult to concentrate, and we have no energy. We can overreact when things don't go our way, and we may find we're less excited if something good happens. So it is easy to see how ongoing sleeplessness can be a worry.

Long term sleep deficiency can increase the risk of chronic health problems such as heart disease and diabetes. It can also significantly affect your mood.

Sleeplessness and mood disorders are closely linked. And it can work both ways – sleep loss can affect your mood, and your mood can affect how much and how well you sleep.

Studies show people who are sleep deprived report increases in negative moods (anger, frustration, irritability, sadness) and decreases in positive moods. And sleeplessness is often a symptom of mood disorders, such as depression and anxiety. It can also raise the risk of, and even contribute to, developing some mood disorders.

Your mood can also affect how well you sleep. Anxiety and stress increase agitation and keep your body aroused, awake and alert. You might find you can't turn your brain off, your heart beats faster and your breathing is quick and shallow.

So getting enough sleep and the right kind of sleep is important.

How much sleep do you need?

How much sleep you need depends on your age, physical activity levels, and general health.

Children and teenagers need 9–10 hours of sleep a night. Younger children tend to go to sleep earlier and wake earlier. As children grow into teenagers, they seem to get tired later and sleep in later.

Adults need around 8 hours sleep each night. We tend to need less sleep, as we get older.

These are some general guidelines. If you (or your children) are tired during the day, you may need more sleep.

Some tips on getting a good night's sleep

If you've been having trouble getting enough good sleep, the good news is there are many ways you can improve your sleep habits. Try these tips:

1. Get a routine and stick to it. Try going to bed around the same time every night and getting up at the same time each morning.
2. Avoid drinking coffee and alcohol too close to bedtime. And finish eating at least two hours before your head hits the pillow.
3. Keep TVs and iPads out of your bedroom.
4. Make your bedroom a haven. Make sure your bed is comfortable. Turn the lights down as you get into bed. Read using a bedside light.
5. Try some simple meditation, like closing your eyes for 5–10 minutes and focusing on taking deep, slow breaths.
6. Enjoy a warm bath.
7. Don't lie awake watching the clock. If you are tossing and turning, try getting up and reading a book for half an hour or so before trying to go to sleep again

The Impact of Sleep on Mood and Mental Well-Being

Have you ever woken up early to start a work week and experienced a profound "case of the Mondays" -- that feeling of drowsiness, lack of energy, irritability, and overall malaise that comes with the start of a new work week. Or has a lack of sleep ever caused you to uncharacteristically snap at a friend or family member over some minor issue? If so, you know from experience what science is now confirming: sleep has a huge impact on our mood and mental well-being.

In both the short and long term, the amount and quality of our sleep can play a huge role in our mental health including how we feel and how we act toward other people. Even just one night of insufficient sleep can bring on stress and a tendency to become easily frustrated. Continued or chronic sleep deprivation can have even more profound effects, significantly impacting a person's overall mood and in some cases leading to issues like depression and anxiety. More and more research is establishing links between depression and insomnia, and because conditions like depression can make it harder to fall asleep, these issues often become part of a self-perpetuating cycle.

Both sleep and mental health are big, complex topics that still require years of dedicated research to better understand. Nevertheless, the more we learn, the more we find that sleep has to be considered a key part of a person's wellness, which includes their physical and emotional health.

In this guide, we'll go into more detail about what is known about sleep and mood and mental well-being. We'll also cover a range of tips that experts agree can help to improve your sleep and put you on the right track to feeling healthier, happier, and well-rested.

What Is the Relationship Between Sleep and Mood?

Mood refers to our emotional state, and mood can be thought of as something that is both general and specific. For example, a person may generally have a positive and happy mood but at times have a mood marked by sadness or anger. How much sleep we get and the quality of that sleep can affect both our general and specific moods.

Not getting enough sleep can contribute to a negative mood. Someone who is sleep deprived is more likely to be sad, irritable, frustrated, stressed out, fatigued, and/or feel similar emotions. This can occur even when sleep is only restricted by a few hours as was found in a study by researchers at the University of Pennsylvania. In that study, participants had their sleep reduced by one-third (to an average of just under 5 hours) for one week. Though studies like this have highlighted how lack of sleep can negatively affect our mood, the odds are that you have dozens of examples from everyday life of seeing how daytime sleepiness can contribute to these negative emotions. If lack of sleep is chronic or persistent, it can take on a greater impact over time.

On the flip side, getting plenty of sleep can contribute to a happier and more positive mood. Even in the study mentioned before, participants generally found that their mood rebounded when they started getting more sleep. Starting your day feeling refreshed can give you more energy, gratitude, and overall pleasantness. This can translate to how you feel during the day and how you go about interacting with other people.

Keep in mind that this impact of sleep on mood is not just about how much you sleep. Though quantity is important, so is sleep quality. If your sleep is fragmented or very light, there's a good chance that you won't get the same kind of mood-related benefits as someone who is getting an equal number of sleep hours but who has smoother progressions through their sleep cycles with fewer interruptions.

How Does Sleep Affect Emotional Reactivity?

Emotional reactivity refers to the situation when our immediate emotional reactions are difficult to control. This can manifest in things like outbursts, withdrawing, lashing out, feeling hurt, or otherwise having limited ability to manage a response to an emotional stimulus. Some people may think of emotional reactivity as defensiveness or the way in which someone may recoil when confronted with an emotional situation.

While some amount of emotional reactivity can be normal from time to time, emotional wellness benefits from being mindful and aware of one's emotions so that they do not become all-encompassing. Unfortunately, poor sleep makes this more difficult as our mood and mental bandwidth are both diminished by lack of sleep. As you've likely witnessed personally at some point in your life, even a person who is usually poised or measured emotionally may be more prone to volatile reactions if they haven't been getting the rest that they need.

Unfortunately, this type of emotional reactivity can stifle communication and short-circuit interpersonal relationships. Emotional reactivity in one person may spur the same in others, making it even more complicated to try to bridge divides to resolve misunderstandings and hurt emotions. This can ultimately lead to harmed relationships and further emotional difficulties.

How Does Insomnia Affect Mental Health?

Insomnia is a broad term that is used to describe difficulty falling asleep, the inability to stay asleep over the course of the night, and/or early morning awakening. When insomnia continues over time, it is called chronic insomnia, and studies have found it to be connected to a number of mental health issues.

Epidemiological studies are those that gather information about health conditions and look for patterns and connections in that data. These studies usually are not able to prove or explain causality, but they can reveal connections that tell us a lot about different health issues. Epidemiological studies, such as those that use regular sleep surveys and health data, have found that there is significant overlap between insomnia and several different mental health disorders including anxiety, depression, ADHD, bipolar disorder, and schizophrenia. This doesn't mean that not getting enough sleep causes those conditions, but it does mean that these issues are found to be co-existing in many patients.

The Bidirectional Relationship Between Sleep and Mental Health Issues

When looking at the relationship between sleep problems like insomnia and mental health, it quickly becomes clear that these problems can be mutually reinforcing. For example, there is evidence that a lack of sleep can increase a person's propensity for anxiety. At the same time, being anxious, including anxious about falling asleep, may prevent someone from getting enough sleep. In this way, these problems can feed into one another and become more difficult to resolve.

Sleep and Anxiety

While anxiety and fear can be totally normal in certain circumstances, in anxiety disorders they become overwhelming and overpowering. Anxiety may be triggered by extremely minor situations and can be paralyzing or debilitating. Studies have found that people who suffer from insomnia are much more likely to struggle with anxiety. Research at the University of California Berkeley found that without adequate sleep, parts of the brain that are related to anxiety tend to become more agitated. This makes people who are prone to anxiety even more likely to be negatively affected by sleep deprivation. As a result, one approach to reducing anxiety in many people is improving sleep quality and quantity,

Sleep and Depression

Depression is a complex condition but can include many symptoms including intense feelings of sadness, lack of energy, limited concentration, excessive daytime sleepiness, insomnia, and others. Many of these symptoms are related to sleep and can be amplified when a person isn't getting enough sleep. Again, this doesn't mean that everyone who has insomnia will become depressed. But there does appear to be a higher incidence of depression in people who have major sleep problems, and these sleep problems also tend to be reinforced as symptoms of depression.

Sleep and Attention-deficit/hyperactivity disorder (ADHD)

Lack of sleep tends to be an issue for many people who have ADHD. This can be a function of the condition itself or many of the medications that may be used to try to help manage ADHD. With fragmented and/or limited sleep, issues of daytime concentration and mood can be further challenged for people with ADHD.

Sleep and Bipolar Disorder

Bipolar disorder is not a common condition in the general population (affecting an estimated 2.8% of adults in the United States), but sleeping problems are normal among people with this diagnosis. People with bipolar disorder have periods of being manic and being depressed, and sleep can be disrupted in both stages. Both can cause insomnia, and during depressed stages, some patients may sleep excessively. Overall, the symptoms of bipolar disorder tend to make it much harder to get a good night's sleep, which can make it even more complicated to try to manage the symptoms of this mental illness.

Sleep and Schizophrenia

People with schizophrenia, which affects around 1% of people in the U.S., tend to have irregular and interrupted sleep. As with the other conditions discussed in this section, this can make it harder to try to address more serious schizophrenic episodes. Some research indicates that by treating sleeping problems in people with schizophrenia, the symptoms of the condition may be reduced.

How Can You Sleep Better to Improve Mood?

Since we know that sleep can have a profound influence on our mood as well as on our overall mental health, it makes sense to try to focus on getting the best sleep possible even if that can at times feel like a challenge. In this section, we'll review some ways that you can try to get the most of each night's sleep.

It Helps to Get Help

Though there are things you can do on your own, improving your mental state and mood with sleep can be enhanced by working with a trained professional. For many mental health issues, working with a counselor or psychiatrist can be of tremendous benefit. Studies have found that talk therapy can reduce the extent of many mental health problems and can also reduce insomnia.

There's even a name for a specific type of talk therapy -- cognitive behavioral therapy for insomnia (CBT-I) -- that helps take on issues like anxiety or depression and their impact on sleep.

It can also be useful to talk with a doctor or nurse especially if you find that you have had other sleep-related issues like chronic snoring or waking up with headaches. Some patients may have an underlying sleep issue like sleep apnea that can be more effectively diagnosed and treated by working directly with a health professional.

Improving Sleep Through Sleep Hygiene

Sleep research has increasingly shown that it's easier to fall asleep and stay asleep if you build the right habits. In general, this is referred to as sleep hygiene, and while it can take some effort and planning, it can really pay off with improving your overall sleep routine. There is no single "best" routine for sleep hygiene, so it's OK to make some modifications based on your own needs and preferences, but general principles of sleep hygiene include:

Go to bed and wake up at consistent times: even during vacations or on weekends, it's advisable to try to go to bed and wake up at the same time. This can help your body adjust to a normal schedule that ideally helps your circadian rhythm be in tune with the local daylight hours.

Follow the same routine before bed: the ideal pre-sleep routine differs for each person, but try to go through the same set of steps every night. This helps strengthen the associations in your mind of this routine and sleeping.

Limit daytime naps: napping for too long or too late in the day can make it much harder to fall asleep when you need to at night.

Build a better bedroom: think about all the aspects of your sleep environment -- light, sound, smells, your mattress, bedding, temperature, etc. -- and work to make your bedroom the most comfortable place possible. If needed, consider products like a new mattress, blackout curtains, a white noise machine, or whatever else is necessary to limit the things that could disrupt your sleep.

Limit screen time: unfortunately, the light and stimulus from your phone (or tablet or laptop) can make it much harder for your mind and body to smoothly transition into sleep. Try to limit screen time leading up to bed and to avoid using these devices in bed.

Find ways to relax: it may be deep breathing or listening to calming music or using aromatherapy, but it can be extremely useful to find a way to relax as you're going to bed. You also likely want to strategize about how you can stay calm if you are struggling to fall asleep or if you wake up unexpectedly in the night.

Build in time for exercise: daily exercise can be beneficial both for improving your sleep and improving your mood and mental health.

It doesn't have to be Olympic-level training, but taking walks or having some regular workouts can dramatically improve your health in a multitude of ways.

Keep a sleep diary: it may be helpful to track what is working and not working for you with regard to your sleep as well as your mood. In a sleep journal, you can take note of your routine, bedtime, wake up time, and how you feel the next day. If you do need to work with a counselor or doctor, this can be very useful information to help them understand your sleep habits and problems.

How to Control Your Emotions so Your Emotions Don't Control You

Sharpening your emotional regulation skills will make you mentally stronger.

Have you ever said something out of anger that you later regretted? Do you let fear talk you out of taking the risks that could really benefit you? If so, you're not alone.

Emotions are powerful. Your mood determines how you interact with people, how much money you spend, how you deal with challenges, and how you spend your time.

Gaining control over your emotions will help you become mentally stronger. Fortunately, anyone can become better at regulating their emotions. Just like any other skill, managing your emotions requires practice and dedication.

Experience Uncomfortable Emotions But Don't Stay Stuck in Them Managing your emotions isn't the same as suppressing them. Ignoring your sadness or pretending you don't feel pain won't make those emotions go away.

In fact, unaddressed emotional wounds are likely to get worse over time. And there's a good chance suppressing your feelings will cause you to turn to unhealthy coping skills--like food or alcohol.

It's important to acknowledge your feelings while also recognizing that your emotions don't have to control you. If you wake up on the wrong side of the bed, you can take control of your mood and turn your day around. If you are angry, you can choose to calm yourself down.

Here are three ways to gain better control over your mood:

1. Label Your Emotions

Before you can change how you feel, you need to acknowledge what you're experiencing right now. Are you nervous? Do you feel disappointed? Are you sad?

Keep in mind that anger sometimes masks emotions that feel vulnerable--like shame or embarrassment. So pay close attention to what's really going on inside of you.

Put a name your emotions. Keep in mind you might feel a whole bunch of emotions at once--like anxious, frustrated, and impatient.

Labeling how you feel can take a lot of the sting out of the emotion. It can also help you take careful note of how those feelings are likely to affect your decisions.

2. Reframe Your Thoughts

Your emotions affect the way you perceive events. If you're feeling anxious and you get an email from the boss that says she wants to see you right away, you might assume you're going to get fired. If however, you're feeling happy when you get that same email, your first thought might be that you're going to be promoted or congratulated on a job well done.

Consider the emotional filter you're looking at the world through. Then, reframe your thoughts to develop a more realistic view.

If you catch yourself thinking, "This networking event is going to be a complete waste of time. No one is going to talk to me and I'm going to look like an idiot," remind yourself, "It's up to me to get something out of the event. I'll introduce myself to new people and show interest in learning about them."

Sometimes, the easiest way to gain a different perspective is to take a step back and ask yourself, "What would I say to a friend who had this problem?" Answering that question will take some of the emotion out of the equation so you can think more rationally.

If you find yourself dwelling on negative things, you may need to change the channel in your brain. A quick physical activity, like going for a walk or cleaning off your desk, can help you stop ruminating.

3. Engage in a Mood Booster

When you're in a bad mood, you're likely to engage in activities that keep you in that state of mind. Isolating yourself, mindlessly scrolling through your phone, or complaining to people around you are just a few of the typical "go-to bad mood behaviors" you might indulge in.

But, those things will keep you stuck. You have to take positive action if you want to feel better.

Think of the things you do when you feel happy. Do those things when you're in a bad mood and you'll start to feel better.

Here are a few examples of mood boosters:

Call a friend to talk about something pleasant (not to continue complaining).
Go for a walk.
Meditate for a few minutes.
Listen to uplifting music.
Keep Practicing Your Emotional Regulation Skills

Managing your emotions is tough at times. And there will likely be a specific emotion--like anger--that sometimes gets the best of you.

But the more time and attention you spend on regulating your emotions, the mentally stronger you'll become. You'll gain confidence in your ability to handle discomfort while also knowing that you can make healthy choices that shift your mood.

How Your Language Patterns Are Tied To Your Emotional Experiences

What is Language Really?

The words you use throughout the day are nothing more than labels you give to your feeling and emotions. They are simply descriptions of your sensory experiences that help you gain a deeper understanding of your life and circumstances. However, these words are only generalizations you make about reality. They don't necessarily describe reality "as it is" but rather describe your understanding of reality as you perceive it to be. Therefore the words you use are simply interpretations you make about things — for better or worse.

You give your experiences "life" with every single word you speak. As such, things don't really have any meaning if you don't take the time to give them a label.

You might for instance label something as being "disgusting" or "delightful". Each label provides a different interpretation of your experience, and each label consequently gives you a very specific kind of feeling. You will, therefore, feel good or bad depending upon the label you give to something. In other words, how you feel at any moment in time is heavily influenced by the words you use to describe your experiences.

Your words are therefore very much assumptions that distort your experience of reality. These assumptions are used to make sense of what's real or ain't real, what's true or isn't true, or what's painful or pleasurable. The key understanding here is that these assumptions are yours and yours alone.

Your words are in ways biased interpretations you make about people, events, and your environment. These interpretations are based on your beliefs, values, self-concept, meta-programs, human needs, psychological rules, thoughts, perspectives, and much more. They are, therefore, in essence, nothing more than psychological anchors we use to induce specific kinds of emotional states.

You experience a particular emotion because the words you use are psychologically anchored to that particular emotion. In other words, each word you speak makes you feel a certain way, and therefore using the "word" itself is a primary reason why you are feeling a certain way at any moment in time. This is, of course, good news and bad news. It's good news because it means that you are fully in control of the emotions you will allow yourself to experience at any moment. However, it's bad news because you normally induce your emotional states without conscious awareness.

The Evolution of Your Language Patterns

Over the course of your life, you have had your ups and downs. You've experienced painful moments, and you've also experienced numerous pleasurable moments. At one time or another, you experienced each of these moments for the very first time. And it's during that "first time" that you made certain assumptions and generalizations about that experience that formed the foundations of your beliefs about "that experience".

At the youngest age, before you even knew how to talk, you would observe the facial expressions of your parents and you would listen to the words they consistently used. Through your observations, you made certain assumptions about what is a painful and what is a pleasurable facial expression. However, you didn't quite know at the time how to verbalize these experiences. But soon that would all change.

As you learned how to speak, you started to give labels to these facial expressions. You also began to label those same emotions within yourself. You would for instance smile, and call that "happy". Or you would frown, and call that "sad". Your facial expressions and other people's facial expressions now had a label, and these labels gave your emotional life more meaning.

As you continued to mature and develop over the years, every facial expression you made and the way you used your body was given a specific kind of label that described that particular state-of-mind. And it's at this early developmental stage that words began to attach themselves to specific kinds of emotions and feelings. These words, in essence, became your emotional anchors. You no longer needed to express yourself through your facial gestures or through your body language to experience the corresponding emotion. Now all you had to do is speak the "word" and you would automatically feel the corresponding emotion. However, there was one problem.

The problem was that the words you spoke "boxed you in" to experiencing things a very specific way. You no longer gave yourself the freedom to allow your body and face to do the "emotionalizing" for you. It was now the words you used that provided the trigger you needed to experience a particular kind of emotional state. These words now formed the foundations of your emotional experiences.

All this might very well be advantageous. After all, communicating through words seems much easier than trying to get that same message across using your body and face. However, you were no longer communicating how you really felt, you were instead labeling your state-of-mind a certain way; thereby triggering a specific kind of emotion. In other words, your verbal language was now directly influencing your state-of-mind, and you, therefore, experienced a certain emotion just because you decided to label your state-of-mind a specific way.

This is all quite significant, however, things become a little more problematic when you consider that the labels you give to certain experiences are based on how you've been conditioned over a lifetime. And how you've been conditioned results from what you've observed and how you've handled pain and pleasure in the past. And the big problem with this is that these labels you give to your experiences might very well have absolutely no basis in reality because the words you use are nothing more than interpretations of experiences that are unique to you, and you alone.

Someone might for instance spill some coffee on you. Based on your past conditioning you might immediately see this as a threat. And a natural response to a threat is to feel angry. And so in your head, you label this incident as something that makes you feel angry, and you, therefore, start yelling at the other person who looks back at you in absolute astonishment.

You learned this response back when you were a child through observing your parents. Your dad might have, for instance, spilled some wine accidentally on your mum's new jeans. She reacted aggressively and started yelling at your dad; telling him how upset and angry she was. And it was this event that shaped your understanding of what it takes to feel angry. And so, years later when someone spills a cup of coffee on your work clothes, you too react in a very similar way by feeling angry about the situation. However, things could have been very different.

What if after your dad had spilled the wine on your mum's jeans, your mum responded in a very understanding manner? That experience would then be ingrained into your psyche, and it would probably take a lot more than a coffee stain to get you feeling angry. This, therefore, suggests that your experience of anger is only your interpretation of reality; and there are certainly other interpretations you could make depending on the labels you give to those experiences.

All this is very significant because every single day you are now giving labels to your life experiences without even giving them a second thought. You respond in anger because you label yourself as feeling angry; you get frustrated because you label yourself as feeling frustrated; you feel stressed because you label yourself as feeling stressed, etc.

It's important to understand that you don't have to feel a certain way about something. You can most certainly choose to feel a very different way about things, however in order to feel differently about things you need to label these experiences in a very different way.

When for instance you think about feeling anxious, at that moment your facial expressions and your body will respond in a certain way that represents an anxious person. However, when you label yourself as feeling excited, then immediately your facial expressions change, your body language transforms, and your expectations shift.

You are no longer feeling anxious because when you label yourself as feeling "excited", this feeling of excitement is already rooted in your psyche in a very specific way. Your body, your facial expressions, and your entire being responds to excitement in a very different way compared to how it responds to anxiety. You have therefore transformed how you will respond to a situation based on the label you have given to that particular experience. And it all started with the language you decide to use.

The Power of a Word

Think of words as something that not only transforms your state-of-mind but also something that changes the course of your entire life.

The verbal language you use literally transforms your experience of reality. It influences your beliefs, evaluations, choices, decisions, perceptions, thoughts, actions, attitude, physiology, habitual patterns, behaviors, etc. In fact, every aspect of your psychology is transformed as a result of the words you choose to use to describe your state-of-mind in any situation. This literally means that your words will essentially determine what you will try or what you will fail to try, which ultimately shapes your expectations and your results moving forward. In other words, your verbal language shapes your destiny — for better or worse.

When for instance you give the label of "fear" to an experience; consider for a moment what comes along with that fear. With fear come certain expectations, beliefs, thoughts, physiological responses, and behaviors. And all these things consequently influence the choices and decisions you will make and the actions you will take moving forward. Therefore, your label of "fear" isn't some isolated psychological event that has no relevance for your future. It's a rather significant event that can dramatically shape your life in immeasurable ways.

What all this suggests is that the words you use to describe your state-of-mind at any moment in time actively shape your destiny. It's therefore absolutely paramount that you get into the habit of transforming your vocabulary in a more positive and helpful way that is in-sync with the type of life you would like to live.

Developing a Rich Vocabulary

One of the significant challenges that most people will have moving forward is that they simply don't have enough words to express how they are truly feeling.

Many people will be familiar with common emotions such as stress, anxiety, worry, anger, overwhelm, frustration, happiness, love, hate, shame, etc. However, there are many more emotions. And because there are many more emotions, there are therefore many different labels you could potentially use to help alter your state-of-mind in any situation.

For instance, please have a look at this list of emotions. Just imagine for a moment having the freedom to describe how you're feeling in so many different ways. What could be the possibilities? How rich would your life be from an emotional perspective?

When you have a limited vocabulary, you live an emotionally impoverished life. On the other hand, when you have a rich vocabulary, you live an emotionally enriching life. And because you have so many ways to describe how you're feeling, you, therefore, have many different ways to perceive and interpret your experiences. And because you have "choice", you can now consciously choose the labels you will use that will best serve you moving forward. You are no longer at the mercy of your limited vocabulary; you are instead the one shaping your life and your destiny with purpose.

Identifying Your Language Patterns

In order to transform your language patterns, you need to first become conscious of the words and phrases you tend to use throughout the day. Furthermore, you need to identify how these patterns are affecting your choices, decisions, and actions. Once you have a clear understanding of how these patterns are influencing your life, you will have the necessary motivation you need to make some positive changes moving forward.

Here is a three-step process that will help you gain some clarity in this area:

Step 1: Examine Your Language Patterns

Let's first begin by analyzing your language patterns. This is not so much about how you talk to others, but rather how you tend to talk to yourself and how you describe the positive and negative experiences in your life.

Have a think about the words you tend to use throughout the day. Specifically, think about the words that cause you the most anguish. These will be words that typically arouse negative feelings and emotions. Ask yourself:

What words do I habitually tend to use each and every day?

What emotions do these words tend to trigger?

Why do these words tend to trigger these particular emotions?

How do these emotions affect me? How do they affect my life?

For the purpose of this exercise, make a list of 20 words that you might typically use that arouse limiting emotional states. However, don't just limit yourself to words alone. You can most certainly list short phrases as well. Although the shorter and more succinct the phrases, the better.

Once you've completed this exercise, feel free to progress to the next step.

Step 2: Bring Your Language Patterns to Conscious Awareness

Your second task is to become consciously aware of how these particular words and phrases developed over a lifetime. We've of course already touched upon this area within the previous section, however, it's important now to take a look at your own life and pinpoint how the words and phrases you consistently use have been conditioned into your psyche.

To begin with, think back to your childhood experiences and recollect how your parents and guardians might have influenced you. Ask yourself:

How did my parents influence these words and phrases?

What influence did my peers have on my vocabulary?

What have my parents and peers got me saying?

How accurate are these labels I give to my experiences?

As you work through these questions, remember to reflect upon the typical words and phrases you identified within Step One of this process.

Now, have a think about the television programs you watch, the music you listen to, the newspapers and books you read and ask yourself:

How has the music I listen to shaped my language patterns?

How has the media shaped my language patterns?

What typical emotions do I tend to experience as a result?

What about the books I read? How have they influenced my language patterns?

Becoming aware of these "influences" will make you more consciously aware and vigilant of your surroundings in the coming days and weeks. You might even start second-guessing some of the words you use to describe certain emotions and experiences. And that's essentially what must happen. Awareness is after all the first step to long-term change and transformation.

Step 3: Assess the Impact of Your Language Patterns
The final step of this process requires identifying the typical language patterns you tend to use throughout the day and the effect that these patterns have on your life. Ask yourself:

What language patterns do I see emerging here?

How do these language patterns shape my beliefs and expectations?

What assumptions do I tend to make as a result of these language patterns?

How are these language patterns affecting the choices and decisions I make?

How are these language patterns ultimately affecting my life?

Are they empowering or limiting me? In what specific way?

Really have a good think about how you use words and phrases throughout the day and how these patterns tend to affect your emotional state-of-mind. The verbal language you use is, after all, shaping your experience of reality. And if you don't appreciate the emotions you experience throughout the day, then maybe it's time you take conscious control and started altering those language patterns with purpose.

Transforming Your Words and Phrases

Throughout the day we all have certain things we say to ourselves without any conscious thought or effort. Most of these words we use are relatively harmless and don't have a great impact on our state-of-mind, on our beliefs, or on our expectations. However, there are certain words and phrases that can actually hurt us.

These language patterns seem kind of harmless on the surface, however, each word and phrase has a hidden agenda that provides you with insight into your true intentions. Consider for a moment words and phrases such as:

I wish...

I should have...

I would have...

I could have...

I can't...

I might...

I have to...

I'll try...

If...

Now, on the surface these words seem rather harmless, however, consider what some of these words imply. For instance, when you say "I should have..." this implies you're feeling guilty. Or, when you say "I could have..." this implies that you're trying to take credit for something. Or, when you say "I can't..." this implies that you're focused on the negatives. Or, when you say "if..." this presupposes you may not. Or, when you say "I'll try..." this implies that you are already making an excuse for failure in advance.

As you can see, what you say may have one meaning on the surface, however, there is a completely different meaning below the surface, and it's this "hidden" meaning that is manifesting at an unconscious level in your life.

The language you use comes attached to a set of beliefs, expectations, psychological rules, etc. All of these aspects of your psyche come to the surface as you use these language patterns, and when they come to the surface they limit your resourcefulness in that particular situation.

It's therefore absolutely paramount that you become consciously aware of the consequences of each word and phrase you use. Furthermore, you must willingly choose to use a different set of words and phrases that will help you to become more resourceful in each situation.

Using Affirmations and Questions

If you're finding this transition difficult, then it might be worthwhile to get into the habit of using affirmations. Affirmations will help you to stay focused on the right things in the right way.

Instead of saying to yourself that "I can't...", choose instead to use a positive affirmation that is stated in a present tense:

I can do this...

I am good at doing this...

This can be done...

This is possible...

I believe in myself...

These affirmations will at the very least focus your mind on more positive outcomes. And when you're focused on more positive outcomes you instantly become more aware of possibilities and opportunities you could potentially take advantage of. These affirmations also make you feel better. You are therefore no longer wallowing in self-pity, but rather focusing on things you can do to help improve your circumstances.

Affirmations do however have their limitations. They are limited because they are passive in nature. They don't actually encourage you to do anything; to make a decision; to take a specific action. However, questions can do this for you quite effectively.

When you ask a question you naturally involve your brain with finding an answer to that question. For instance, instead of saying "I can't...", choose to ask the following set of questions:

What if I could do this?

If I could do this, how would I go about doing it?

What would be possible if...?

How would another person do this successfully?

What small thing could I do right now that could prove to me that I can get this started?

As you ask these questions you are already engaged and searching for answers. Of course, you might not immediately acquire the answers you are after. And that's perfectly okay. If you don't have the answers, then ask a different set of questions that can help you acquire these answers. In fact, the more questions you ask, the better you will feel because more questions bring about more possibilities, and when you have more possibilities you have more options available moving forward.

It's also important to note that every question you ask makes you more resourceful. And the more resourceful you become the better questions you will ask, and the more answers you will have that can help you work through your circumstances successfully.

To gain more insights about questions, please have a read of How to Ask Better Questions.

Consciously Choosing Your Words

Have a think for a moment about the words you typically use on a daily basis and the negative emotions that are often associated with those words. Now imagine NEVER AGAIN using those words in your life. Ask yourself:

What if I never used this word ever again in my life?

Without this word in my vocabulary would I ever feel the emotion that this word represents?

Maybe the emotion would be less intense or different without this word?

How would my state-of-mind change without ever saying or thinking this word?

Of course not using one particular word might force you to use another word to describe what you're experiencing or feeling. And this is perfectly understandable. It's all about letting go of those negative and limiting words that put you in a very poor state-of-mind. These are the words that you must eradicate from your vocabulary.

Consider for a moment:

What emotions would I never want to experience again?

What kinds of words represent these emotional experiences?

What alternate words could I potentially use to label these experiences?

Think through all the negative emotions you ever experienced and write down the words you typically use to label those emotions. Now, cross these words out with a pen and write down alternate words you could use that describe those same emotional experiences. Keep in mind though that you have two options you can select from:

Option 1: Replace the negative words with words of a lower negative intensity.
Option 2: Replace the negative words with positive words.
Here are some examples:

Change ANGRY to passionate or disenchanted.
Change AFRAID to uncomfortable.
Change CONFUSED to curious.
Change SICK to cleansing.
Change NERVOUS to energized or excited.
Change FRUSTRATED to fascinated.

Change FAILURE to learning.

Change EXHAUSTED to recharging.

Change DISAPPOINTED to delayed.

Now consider for a moment what eliminating all those capitalized words from your vocabulary would mean to you. Not only will you not feel those emotions as you have felt them in the past, but you will now become more resourceful than ever before.

For instance, instead of feeling frustrated you now describe "frustration" as fascination. This is advantageous because when you're fascinated you think differently about the situation, you ask better questions, you have different expectations, etc. You essentially become a very different person in this situation just because you "flicked the switch" from frustration to fascination.

Or, let's take a look at another example from this list. Imagine you eliminated the word "failure" from your vocabulary. What would be the significance of this? Well, for starters consider how you feel when you label yourself as a failure:

Do you feel upset?

Do you feel miserable?

Do you feel inadequate or incapable?

What else might you feel?

Now, think about how you feel when you are in a state of learning:

Do you feel curious?

Do you feel excited?

Do you feel intelligent?

What else might you feel?

Given all this, which state-of-mind do you think would be more appropriate to experience in any situation? Of course, that answer would be a "learning" state-of-mind. Why? Because when you're in a state of "learning" you naturally become more positive and resourceful. You no longer pity yourself or think about how miserable your life was when you labeled yourself as a failure. Instead, you are now asking better questions, you are looking at expanding your horizons, you are grasping for new opportunities and experiences, etc.

The possibilities are literally endless. And the best news about all this is that in a state of learning you access a different set of beliefs that are built upon the idea of "learning". These beliefs are certainly not accessible when you label yourself as a failure because from a "failure" mentality there are no empowering beliefs. All beliefs built upon the idea of failure are there to bring you down emotionally and discourage further effort. And that certainly isn't an optimal way to live your life.

Some Words of Caution

Some words or phrases you use might be deeply ingrained in your psyche. In fact, they are so deeply entrenched, that even thinking about using another word or phrase can create an incredible amount of internal resistance. It may even bring-up all these limiting beliefs to the surface that make it very difficult for you to put yourself into a more positive state-of-mind.

In such instances, you should tone down the changes you are making. Therefore, instead of transforming a negative word or phrase into a positive word or phrase, choose to replace that negative word with another word that is of a lower negative intensity. For instance, you could turn "I'm feeling angry" into:

I'm feeling a little irritated.

I'm feeling somewhat uncomfortable.

I'm feeling rather disenchanted.

Each of these words still "border" on the negative side, however they are not filled with as much emotional intensity as "anger", which means that you will not experience as much resistance to these words as you would if you interpreted your anger in a positive way, e.g. "I am feeling passionate". In this instance, "passion" might be a little too far of a stretch.

Over time as you feel more comfortable using these "less intense" words, you can switch to using more positive words that will allow you to become even more resourceful in these kinds of situations. It's all about making progressive change that is believable over an extended period of time. However, if you would like to make more rapid changes then please have a read of How to Transform Limiting Beliefs.

Now, as a final exercise in this section, go back to the list of emotions and write down all the words you could potentially use that could replace your current emotional language patterns. After which, immediately start putting these new words to use. It would be interesting to hear how you go.

How To change your emotions

Experiences get stored in our brains just like files get stored in the folders of a computer. Once you recall a certain experience your mind will access the folder that contains all similar experiences and as a result your emotions will intensify.

Do you remember how you felt the last time a friend annoyed you?

Most probably you started remembering all of the bad things that he did to you before and maybe you also started remembering all the similar bad things that other people did to you.

Our memories are selective, this means that we only remember the things that we want to remember depending on the emotions we are experiencing. When you felt angry your selective memory started to recall all situations that made you angry in the past and that's why your anger became more intense.

Now what if few minutes later your friend called you and told you that he is sorry and that he didn't mean to annoy you. At this point your selective memory will let you recall the good things that this person did to you before and it will prevent you from remembering the bad things that he did.

When your emotions changed your mind accessed a different folder inside your brain that contains all the good things that this person did.

So how can you use such information to change your emotions?

Changing your emotions

The starting point of your thoughts is extremely important because its the one that will determine which folder your mind is going to access. If your initial thought was negative then most probably you will start recalling more negative thoughts and you will end up feeling really bad.

In order to change your emotions you need to make sure that you use some kind of a trigger that can help you access the right folder in your brain.

So how can you do this?

1) Take a powerful action: Sometimes you need to take an action while you are feeling bad in order to change your emotions to the better. In many cases you wont be able to change your emotions before you take a certain action, For example if you were procrastinating since a long time then suddenly you started doing the things that you always wanted to do then within few days your mind will be forced into the positive area and your emotions will be changed to positive ones

2) Create the starting point I am sure that there is some kind of music that can help you feel good or at least help you get one positive thought. Listening to such music can be the trigger that forces your mind into the positive track. This trigger can extend to include talking to certain people, visualizing certain goals or recalling your big dreams. Just use whatever trigger you can use to trigger positive thoughts

3) Avoid the wrong triggers As you now know one negative thought can force you to recall all the other related negative thoughts that's why you should always do your best to avoid negative triggers such as negative people, negative self talk or negative media

Changing your emotions and taking actions
Some people think that all what they need to do to feel good or to change their emotions to the better is to think positively or use affirmations. While these methods can have a temporary effect on their moods sooner or later their life problems will force them to think negatively and as a result their emotions will change to the worse.

Most people mistakenly think that their emotions are the starting point of their bad moods while in fact they are just the result of the unsolved life problems they didn't deal with.

If you kept ignoring your goals and dreams while thinking positively then sooner or later your subconscious mind will send you bad emotions in order to motivate you to peruse your goals.

If you really want to change your emotions then apply what you read in this article while taking serious actions to solve your life problems.

How Music Affects Your Emotion

From the drumbeats of our ancient ancestors to today's unlimited streaming services, music is an integral part of the human experience.

Researchers have pondered the possible therapeutic and mood boosting benefits of music for centuries.

Even sad music brings most listeners pleasure and comfort, according to recent research from Durham University in the United Kingdom and the University of Jyväskylä in Finland

Conversely, the study found that for some people, sad music can cause negative feelings of profound grief.

The research involved three surveys of more than 2,400 people in the United Kingdom and Finland, focusing on the emotions and memorable experiences associated with listening to sad songs.

The majority of experiences reported by participants were positive. From the drumbeats of our ancient ancestors to today's unlimited streaming services, music is an integral part of the human experience.

Researchers have pondered the possible therapeutic and mood boosting benefits of music for centuries.

Even sad music brings most listeners pleasure and comfort, according to recent research from Durham University in the United Kingdom and the University of Jyväskylä in Finland, published in PLOS ONE.

Conversely, the study found that for some people, sad music can cause negative feelings of profound grief.

The research involved three surveys of more than 2,400 people in the United Kingdom and Finland, focusing on the emotions and memorable experiences associated with listening to sad songs.

The majority of experiences reported by participants were positive.

"The results help us to pinpoint the ways people regulate their mood with the help of music, as well as how music rehabilitation and music therapy might tap into these processes of comfort, relief, and enjoyment," said lead author, Tuomas Eerola, Ph.D., a professor of music cognition at Durham University, in a press release.

He also said the study may help find reasons for both listening to and avoiding sad music.

An earlier study, published in the Journal of Consumer Research, found that people tend to prefer sad music when they are experiencing a deep interpersonal loss, like the end of a relationship.

The authors of that study suggested that sad music provides a substitute for the lost relationship. They compared it to the preference most people have for an empathic friend — someone who truly understands what you're going through.

Other research has focused on the joy upbeat music can bring.

A 2013 study in the Journal of Positive Psychology found that people who listened to upbeat music could improve their moods and boost their happiness in just two weeks.

In the study, participants were instructed to try to improve their mood, but they only succeeded when they listened to the upbeat music of Copland as opposed to the sadder tunes of Stravinsky.

And a happier mood brings benefits beyond feeling good. In a press release, lead study author, Yuna Ferguson, noted that happiness has been linked to better physical health, higher income, and greater relationship satisfaction.

Read more: The music you choose may say something about your mental health »

Music as therapy
This music research aligns with the larger arena of music therapy.

The American Music Therapy Association (AMTA) reports that music therapy programs can be designed to achieve goals such as managing stress, enhancing memory, and alleviating pain.

It might seem surprising that music can help people cope with physical pain, but research has shown a clear link.

A 2015 review in The Lancetfound that people who listened to music before, during, or after surgery experienced less pain and anxiety, compared to patients who did not listen to music.

The music listeners didn't even need as much pain medication.

To conduct the study, researchers looked at data from 73 different trials, involving more than 7,000 patients.

The people who experienced a slightly greater, but nonsignificant, reduction in pain, and needed the least pain medication, were the ones who got to pick their own music.

"Music is a non-invasive, safe, cheap intervention that should be available to everyone undergoing surgery," lead study author Catherine Meads, Ph.D., of Brunel University in the United Kingdom, recommended in a press release.

When it comes to treating chronic conditions, music therapy can also play a powerful role.

A recent review in the World Journal of Psychiatry found that music therapy can be an effective treatment for mood disorders related to neurological conditions, including Parkinson's disease, dementia, stroke, and multiple sclerosis.

After reviewing 25 trials, the researchers concluded that music is a valid therapy to potentially reduce depression and anxiety, as well as to improve mood, self-esteem, and quality of life.

They also noted that no negative side effects were reported in any of the trials, making music a low-risk treatment.

Barry Goldstein, a recording artist who has studied the vibrational effects of music for more than 25 years, says music has a profound impact on the brain.

In a column for Conscious Lifestyle magazine, Goldstein wrote that music can actually enhance brain functions.

He said music can evoke emotion, help regain memories, stimulate new neural connections, and active attention.

7 Ways Music Affects Your Mood And Emotions

Music is an all present aspect of the world culture. There is no archaeological evidence its true origins. But between 60,000 and 30,000 years ago, humans made paintings in the caves and jewelry among other things. These new behaviors let scientists presume that music also appeared during this period as the result of stated intentionality.

Evolutionary scientists think that music was one of the reasons prehistoric human survived. They believe that its influence on emotions helped the communication among people and integration in the group. "The emotional response people have to music is basically predicted by two main factors," Professor Adrian North, at Curtin University. "The first is whether it's considered to be pleasant or unpleasant, and the second is how 'active' versus 'sleepy' the music is."

1. Affects the brain

Neuroscientists now know that music influences different parts of the brain. This is one of the reasons why some professionals use it to treat anxiety disorders and depression. Hippocampus, prefrontal cortex and parietal lobe are the parts of the brain that are responsible for emotions and moods.

For example, prefrontal cortex, which is also known as "seat of good judgment", is in charge of extreme impulses. It enables good decisions in order to prevent the unacceptable behaviors. Due to these properties, music was part of a number of therapies, like in stroke patients who learned to speak. Also, speech therapists recommend it as a therapy for stuttering.

2. A mood lifter

People turn to music when they're experiencing any emotional turmoil. They see it as a way to lift their mood and feel better. This is because it encourages the production of serotonin – a happiness hormone. The calming tones also engulf the body with dopamine which is a neurotransmitter responsible for feeling good. Another important hormone released through music is norepinephrine which creates euphoria.

All these hormones are important for treating depression and anxiety disorder. Knowing how the music influences the production of these substances facilitates therapies for these mental states. Some scientists even believe that music can replace antidepressants in some instances. A 2013 study in the Journal of Positive Psychology found it only takes two weeks for people to recover from bad mood if they're listening to upbeat music.

In the UK, the scientists from the Bournemouth University Dementia Institute (BUDI) have started research project called the orchestra. Its purpose is to show how patients with dementia can learn new skills. Eight demented patients participated in the project, as did students and professional musicians.

"Music touches everyone in some way, either by listening or playing," said Anthea Innes, Ph.D., head of BUDI. "Working together to produce a collaborative output is a powerful way to bring out the best in people — not just in terms of their musical skills, but their communication skills, friendships, care, and support for one another," she added.

3. A motivator

It's all about the type of message the music is sending. Songs with inspirational motives can have a positive effect and make you feel better. The message and joy when singing are the motivators to pull yourself up and regain control of your surroundings. That's why it's recommended to listen to uplifting songs with strong meaning and motivational power. When it comes to the message, the words and tune must be in sync and jointly encourage positive actions.

4. Reduces stress levels

Music is a practical stress reliever. It can affect the tense muscles and help them relax with its calming tunes. Also, it can reduce your breathing rate and thus slow down your heart. These are all the science of relaxing and calming down.

It is believed that listening to classical music can have a specific soothing effect on the body and mind. Additionally, singing along is a great way to mitigate tension. In Japan, people use karaoke to manage stress and tension. Soothing music is, also, perfect to help you sleep and relax you before the bedtime.

5. Changes perception

When people are sad, they tend to cling to the cause of that sadness for a certain period. In order to move on and look at the bright side of life, people use music. It has the power to change the way we perceive reality and help us see other, positive aspects. Even though we usually see in movies that depressed people listen to the sad songs, that has the drowning effect. Therefore, turning up the volume of a livelier tune can change your perception for the better, believe the scientists.

6. Influences memory

Music is commonly used for the treatment of Alzheimer's disease. It helps the brain to regain some memories and even improves its health. By playing music the patients' used to love, it is possible to elevate their mood and help them become aware of the world. It makes them aware and able to communicate, as well as to reconnect with parts of their life they have forgotten.

A 2009 study by Petr Janata at the University of California found that there is a part of our brains which connect music and memories. This is triggered when we listen to emotionally significant songs from our past.

7.   Used as therapy

The American Music Therapy Association says that stress, pain, and loss of memories can be managed with therapy programs based on music. In 2015, The Lancet published an article on the study about how it influenced people who were going through surgery. Namely, those who listened to music before, during and after the surgery felt less pain and nervousness, compared to those who didn't.

This study included a review of data from 73 different clinical trials involving over 7,000 subjects. Those who chose their music experienced less pain and needed less medication. "Music is a non-invasive, safe, cheap intervention that should be available to everyone undergoing surgery," said the lead study author Catherine Meads, Ph.D., of Brunel University in the UK.

The article in the World Journal of Psychiatry addressed the effectiveness of music therapy for treatment of neurological conditions, like dementia, stroke, Parkinson's disease and multiple sclerosis. Themes and variations influence the brain areas which are responsible for mood improvement, self-esteem and quality of lifestyle. This was the conclusion after the scientists reviewed 25 clinical trials examining the validity of music therapy for reduction of anxiety and depression.

It's important to mention that there were no negative effects during the trials which make music therapy a low-risk treatment. Due to these findings, many scientists believe it has the potential to enhance brain functions.

Music is widely available and that makes it a perfect remedy for people going through psychological problems. There are many streaming services today which allow us to access it from any place and at any time. If the neuroscience continues working on the way to improve the positive effects of music on the brain, medicines might become obsolete. Also, people would much easily accept this way of therapy and feel more comfortable with its principles.

Cultivating Positive Emotions

Ten emotional seeds to plant in your garden now.

Think of your mind, your emotions and your spirit as the ultimate garden. The way to ensure a bountiful, nourishing harvest is to plant seeds like love, warmth and appreciation — instead of seeds of disappointment, anger and fear.

Here are 10 emotional seeds to plant in your garden now. Use them to bring fulfillment and abundance to your life, and as an antidote to negative emotions.

Gratitude

Gratitude is the single greatest power to change your life. Spiritual leaders and philosophers across the world credit a happier life to it. Deepak Chopra describes gratitude as an "immensely powerful force that we can use to expand our happiness, create loving relationships, and even improve our health." As Tony says, "When you are grateful, fear disappears and abundance appears."

Hunger

In a LinkedIn article Tony addressed the emotion most essential to success: "If someone asks me, "Tony what is the single most valuable secret to success in life? How do I live life on my terms and have choices, and become the best in my field?" I'd tell them that every great leader I've ever had the privilege to work with – whether they are a politician an athlete, a musician or a business savant – got there using one force above all other. And that's hunger." If you are going to create lasting value in the world, you must have the determination to make change happen.

Passion

Passion is a force that awakens you. Passion blows the lid off of your imagination, your capability and your drive. It shakes your mind free from limiting beliefs and breaks your old patterns of thinking. Passion is what gives you a sense of purpose. Excitement and passion can add "juice" to just about anything. To paraphrase Benjamin Disraeli, "man is only truly great when he acts from passion."

Love and warmth

The consistent expression of love can melt almost any negative emotion it comes in contact with. Recognize that whether you are met with an expression of love or a cry for help, the intent is positive. Recognizing the positive intent within yourself and others allows you to be gracious rather than offended.

Curiosity

If you really want to grow in life, learn to be as curious as a child. Children know how to wonder – to marvel at things most obvious or routine to the average adult. That's why they're rarely bored! When you're curious, nothing is a chore.

Flexibility

The ability to change what's going on – to adapt rapidly and without getting upset – is the guarantee of success. Your level of happiness is in direct proportion to the amount of uncertainty you are willing to live with. As Amazon founder Jeff Bezos once said, "We are stubborn on vision. We are flexible on details."

Confidence

When you're confident, you are willing to experience the power of faith – the trust that things will work out. Unshakable confidence provides the sense of certainty we all want.

Cheerfulness

Being cheerful means you live life in a state of pleasure – one that's so intense that you transmit a sense of joy to those around you.

Vitality

Vitality – or energy – is our life force. Your mental or emotional state starts with your energy level. Remember when you were a kid and you would run into a room or splash through a puddle, and you felt full of life? Well, the ultimate source of energy is our psychology. You can choose to be in an "energy rich" state of mind.

Sense of contribution

Only those who have learned the power of sincere and selfless contribution experience life's deepest joy: true fulfillment. If every day you can feel that what you do adds something not only to your own life, but to others as well, then life takes on a new, deeper sense of meaning. There's no richer emotion than the sense that who you are as a person, something you've said or done, has added to the life of someone you care about or perhaps someone you don't even know.

Develop Awareness

There are some key areas, four actually, to lead you to success in personal development and they all have to do with awareness. Awareness, realizing that you have the choice about what happens in your life. Get to be aware of:

how you feel each day
how you behave
which people and situations you attract to your life
what meanings you assign to things
What to do with the awareness?

Once you are aware you can choose these on a minute by minute, the next step is to direct your attention to the most effective places to put it. If you're interested in personal development, then you realize where you direct your attention matters. You can become an extraordinary person by choosing your awareness.

So, an example of using awareness is in seminars. People go to a seminar and get pumped up and excited. They experience the "seminar high" for days after. A good seminar leader uses pictures and thoughts to get the attendees to focus on. These are all of things they want and think are possible to attain. The brain releases endorphins that cause you the feeling of greatness, invincible, the "can do" high.

The teacher does certain things to cause the focus to be on the positive. However, when the seminar is over, and everyone is back home in their own environment, and go back to their previous internal set point. Until the next seminar, where they go and get another seminar hit.

What you really want to do is develop your awareness. See how you are creating the high. That "high" feeling leads to actions which creates results. Its about creating your awareness, internal and external. There is a price to pay for the ability to create, most people aren't willing to pay. They would rather go to a seminar to get their "fix". They are not motivated to do it for themselves though they know what they need to do.

How Do You Develop The Correct Attitude?

As long as the "high" is being done outside of yourself, its done on autopilot, and you have no control over it. Instead do meditation (use holosync technology to get faster results)and then become aware of the 4 areas of awareness spoken about here. If you develop your choice about these, then you can create anything you want.

Yes, there are many things we have no control over - the sun rising and setting; tornadoes and hurricanes; control over other people and their agendas that are different than yours. By becoming aware, you can avoid the things you cannot change.

Every problem with being a human that can be solved, the solution is supplied by awareness. If you are aware enough, you'll be able to have the maximum choice on how you feel and how you behave. You will also be aware enough to realize which things you cannot change. Embrace that.

How Do You Develop Awareness

Awareness is actually very easy to develop. All you have to do is stop worrying about the past, don't anticipate a future that hasn't occurred and stay focused on your thoughts and actions in this very moment.

OUCH! That may seem next to impossible for many people.

The reason is conditioning. Most people are so consumed by the past and future that they miss the beauty of every moment they are actually living.

Think about that for a moment. Whenever you are stuck and thinking about anything except right now, this moment, you are truly missing the richness of every "now" you are actually living.

This moment is all that you can control. The past flavors your actions today with the wisdom of experience and your future is created by the thoughts and actions you take right now.

What kind of future are you creating today?

Recondition your thinking by simply catching yourself slipping into the familiar patterns of past or future thinking.

Catching yourself is easier than you might think. It just takes awareness of what you are thinking in any given moment.

Take this eBook for example. You are reading it, probably thinking of something you have to do, wish you did, or are putting off for some future "better" time.

What about your thoughts right now, as you read this?

STOP for a moment and consider what you are thinking as you read these words. Write down any ideas that you will apply to your life.

When you interrupt your old thought patterns with a big bold STOP, you are conditioning your mind to listen to your true desires and not run rampant on its own, creating confusion, stress and overwhelm.

3-fun things you can do to develop greater awareness

1. Play a round of golf. Notice what you are thinking about between shots, as you hover over the ball anticipating your next shot, or as you line up a putt. It is probably focused on what already happened or what will/may happen.

STOP, catch yourself, focus on the feeling you'll have when you make a great shot, then take the shot. For every poor shot you hit, be aware of your actual thoughts. I'll bet those past and future thoughts crept in there.

2. Sit quietly with a pen and paper and write down anything that comes to mind in the moment you are sitting there.

If you start thinking about the past or the future STOP, reframe, and focus on right now.

When you are just sitting peacefully and not thinking of anything except right now, what thoughts do you have? Write them down, then read and reflect on them.

3. Go into nature with a camera. Don't look for the obvious sweeping vistas. Instead look for tiny little miracles all around you like the way the sunlight plays off of a flower, the way a rock sits in a stream, the beauty of the bark on a tree, or the miracle of a blade of grass.

Notice things you seldom allow yourself to see and take a photo of them. What did you notice that you have overlooked before? How did that make you feel? Write down your feelings as you review the photos you took.

Take the awareness you gained in the exercises above and apply them to your life in business.

When you are getting ready to launch a new marketing campaign or create a new sales push how do you feel? Are you focused on results of the past or future or are you experiencing how great you'll feel when your campaign succeeds?

Remember the great golf shot. Didn't you make your best shots when you envisioned the outcome you really wanted?

When you are stuck with a business problem do you panic and scramble for answers or are you calmly analyzing the situation; allowing your mind to peacefully explore and find new ideas that solve old challenges?

Remember how great it felt to relax and explore your feelings and thoughts in a given moment.

How about when are looking for new ways to grow your revenues. Are you aware only of the obvious sweeping vistas?

Remember the small miracles that you discovered simply by looking for them. Awareness is a state of mind. It is focused on right here and now, instead of a past or a future.

The creative mind is aware of everything. It's your past/future panic thoughts that comes in to block the beauty of this moment; keeping you stuck in the realm of confusion instead of open to the beauty of your personal genius in this very moment.

Being Emotionally Intelligent

Our natural state of being, as one with Soul, is a harmonious state of Love, in which the only feelings are of continuous peace and bliss. Therefore if we are feeling any feeling other than peace and bliss, we have got out of balance somewhere. This is due to our conditioned and faulty thinking, which emerges as tolerations, needs and limiting beliefs. Using our Emotional Intelligence equips us to identify the message that Soul is sending us through these feelings, so we can rectify our thinking and thus move always towards Love.

Being Emotionally Intelligent is my ability to consciously comprehend my own emotional States of Being. Being 'Emotional' means that I am aware of the feeling that is my emotional state of being. Being 'Intelligent' means I have a rational knowledge or logical understanding of the situation, occurrence and circumstances that I am currently experiencing. I am Intelligent when I can consciously rationalise what is happening in my reality. I am Emotional when I can feel the awareness of my energetic state of being - my emotional energy.

Emotional Intelligence loses clarity when I confuse 'being emotional' with 'being irrational'. When I am studying negative states of being that cause me to sub-consciously react, I am learning about my own irrational behaviour that is without emotional intelligence. I am studying 'irrational intelligence'.

Being emotional is not reacting irrationally; it is being consciously-aware of my emotional state of being. I never react emotionally because with emotional intelligence I am always able to respond intelligently. Negative emotional states of being are irrational because a rationally intelligent person who is emotionally aware (intelligent) would never choose to experience them. Understanding irrational behaviour does require emotional intelligence but it is not the definition of Emotional Intelligence.

Emotional States of Being

Emotional 'States of Being' require definition before I can understand them intelligently. When I define an emotional state of being, I give it definition, it becomes a definite emotion, and I become consciously-aware of its existence.
It is my conscious-awareness of the definite nature of my emotions that allows me to be emotionally intelligent.

An 'Emotional' person is aware of their feelings as different emotions.

An 'Emotionally Intelligent' person is able to consciously name (define) their emotional state of being and create it at will, if and when they so choose.By intelligently defining an emotion, I become both emotionally aware of the feeling and rationally conscious of its definition. I cannot experience a definite emotion unless I can name it adjectively. In the absence of naming an emotion, it will remain either a positive or a negative experience, dependent on the beliefs that I hold in my sub-conscious.

I define an emotion (emotional state of being) with an adjective, which is a describing word. Any adjective that describes my feelings or my emotional state of being is an emotion.Without an adjective to describe it, an emotion is just a feeling that I don't really understand.

The Potential of my Emotional Energy

Emotion is an energetic state of being that I am experiencing. All forms of energy have a force, a magnitude and a potential. Emotions are no different. The potential of any energy is realised when the force and magnitude of that energy unite.

Electrical energy has a force called 'volts', a magnitude called 'amps' and a potential called 'watts'. They are all named after the person who first defined them. Emotional energy is more complicated because not only is its potential divided by force and magnitude but its force is divided by polarity and its magnitude is divided by gender.

The polarity of my emotions is either positive or negative and the gender of my energy is either male or female. (Anger & pride are male whereas meekness & humility are female. However, Impatience and intolerance are usually seen as negative and patience and tolerance as positive).

The degree, to which my emotional energy is unbalanced, by being divided by either polarity or gender or both, determines the intensity of the emotion that I am feeling. The greater is the imbalance the greater is the intensity of the emotional feeling. The intensity of my emotional state of being is the product of both the gender and the polarity of the emotional energy.

Emotional Intelligence requires not only the definition of my emotional state of being but the understanding of its potential for my Life.

Understanding the potential of my emotional energy requires me to be consciously-aware of:

o Its force and magnitude

o Its gender, polarity and intensity

o Its definition or Adjectivity

o The sponsoring thought or thoughts that are creating the emotion. The Ultimate Potential of my Emotional Energy is the Pure Feeling of Love that emanates from my Soul.

Life is an emotional experience

My Emotional Intelligence requires more than my ability to manage my irrational behaviour. It requires the ability to understand my emotional experiences intelligently.The cause of my irrational behaviour is my lack of emotional intelligence. I react irrationally with what is sometimes confusingly called an emotional reaction.

I respond with positive emotion once I attain the intelligence and understanding to do so. My symptoms of irrational behaviour are created by my lack of rational intelligence. Extreme irrational behaviour caused by a lack of rational ability may be diagnosed as a mental illness by a rational person who has no emotional intelligence.

Diagnosing emotional disorder or disease requires emotional intelligence not rational intelligence, which is probably why illness is usually diagnosed as either physical or mental and not emotional. In the absence of emotional intelligence, my life became an unemotional experience as a rationally intelligent man.

In a dualistic world, the more rationally intelligent I become the more contained, disconnected and emotionally unintelligent I am. It is my experience that the more I rationalise my world with tolerance and patience the less I react with the frustration of my anger and intolerance. However, with emotional intelligence I consciously choose to be 'Accepting' instead of tolerant and 'Allowing' instead of patient. I no longer choose to be a tolerant patient who is patiently tolerating Life.

I am now accepting Life as an emotional experience because I am learning to be emotionally intelligent enough to allow it to be so.

The True Test of Emotional Intelligence

The true test of my Emotional Intelligence is whether I can be Happy & Well as a result of my conscious choice to be so. It is only my emotional ignorance that is depriving me of the happiness and well-being that is my true nature.

Happiness is an emotional feeling. How can a rational man be happy in a state of being disconnected and unemotional? Well-being is an emotional feeling. How can I feel well in a society that medicates physical and mental illness without one iota of emotional intelligence?

Having compassion for other people doesn't mean anything unless I have defined the compassion that I am feeling. Defining compassion as: "Wanting to alleviate the suffering of others", is a rationally intelligent definition of a physical desire not the definition of an emotional feeling.

It is my lack of emotional intelligence that disconnects me from my true emotional nature. A logical world has become an unemotional world that is devoid of true Happiness & Well-being and is full of sadness and sickness. We have lost our connection to our true Wealth and our true Health when, as a society, we are disconnected from our Emotional Intelligence.

In an emotionally intelligent society, the only irrational behaviour is to be unemotional and intellectually challenged by one's own emotional experiences. The challenge of a new society is for men to become emotionally-rational and for women to become rationally-emotional and for both to understand that there is no distinction between the two. The battle of the Sexes will then be declared as over.

How to Transform Emotional Upset Into Empowered Action

While we like to think of ourselves as rational beings, in reality our lives are ruled by emotions. Emotions upset us, drive us, intimidate us, and inspire us. They move us to action or paralyze us in anxiety, stress, and fear. For this reason, it's natural to be somewhat wary of emotions-and do what we can to avoid them or keep them at bay.

Yet, because of the real power of emotions, learning to understand and relate to your emotions in a more conscious, intentional, and empowered way is essential to living a life of greater peace, love, success, enjoyment, and purpose.

Here are 3 keys to transform your emotional experience.

Emotional Key #1: Reset the Biology of Your Emotions

Psychiatrist Dr. Judith Orloff says that "All emotions trigger biological reactions that shape your health just as distinctly as what you choose to eat or how you choose to exercise... how you react emotionally is a choice in any situation-and those choices can make or break your chances for well-being." (p.34, Emotional Freedom)

For example, when you emotionally react with worry, anxiety, and fear this triggers a stress response in your body. Stress hormones shoot through you, inhibiting your higher brain functions, elevating your heart rate and respiration, shunting blood away from your internal organs to your limbs, and shutting down your immune system in favor of sending energy to your muscles for action.

If these conditions of stress persist long-term, your body will begin to break down. You will not perform even the most basic functions such as breathing and digestion efficiently or effectively. Chronic stress also inhibits your ability to think clearly, create solutions, and relate to others with compassion.

Therefore, it's absolutely essential that you learn to counter your body's stress reaction by cultivating conscious relaxation and inner peace. Whether this is by taking a break and going for a walk in nature, taking time for recreation with your loved ones, or by learning and practicing the skills of meditation, it's absolutely essential that you take an active role to shift your body out of stress mode when strong emotions arise.

Emotional Key #2: Uncover The Deeper Meaning Of Your Emotions

While it's essential to learn to calm and relax yourself, it is just as important not to shove your emotions aside. Your emotions are an invaluable source of information, once you learn to read their language. Within each emotional experience is a seed for greater self-awareness and higher learning.

So, when you begin to feel emotions of any kind, and especially "negative" ones, pause to ask yourself, "What am I being shown in this situation? How can I learn, grow, and evolve through this experience?"

To do that, you'll first have to become aware of the specific emotion you are feeling. This requires accepting what you are feeling completely, without judgment. Not always an easy task.

However, see if you can take a step back and just notice what you're feeling. See if you can break your sense of identification with it. In other words, understand your emotion as information, not as defining who you are.

When we identify ourselves with our emotions, we are caught up in and swept away by them. We ride on the rollercoaster of emotion, which can feel scary and out of control.

Instead, see if you can label your emotion and notice it as a sensation in your body. See if you can take an investigative approach. Become curious. As you do that, you may notice that you can feel into your emotions without being consumed by them.

What if your life is like a laboratory and your emotional experiences are the raw data? See if you can recognize patterns in the data of your feelings, understand what prompts them, and see what they are asking you to realize, do, or overcome.

When you show acceptance and compassion to yourself within your own emotional experiences, you'll naturally begin to accept and have compassion for others in their emotional experiences, as well.

Emotions are here to teach us to move beyond our small sense of ourselves into deeper love and wisdom. As you learn to discover the meaning and purpose of your emotions, they become messages that guide your life.

Emotional Key #3: Use the Energy in your Emotions

While emotions contain meaningful messages, they also come with energy to do something. This is true for so-called "negative" emotions as well as "positive" ones. For example:

ANGER arises when you, or someone or something you love, is threatened and you need to take protective action or set a firm boundary.

SADNESS arises when you need to let go of what no longer serves you or what is past, so you can move forward.

FEAR arises to prompt you to take preventative action.

JOY prompts you toward expansive, expressive, creative action.

COMPASSION prompts you to care for others.

So, every emotion has a MESSAGE and ENERGY to carry out a specific type of action. Understanding your emotions helps you to receive those messages and take those actions.

So, as emotions come up, instead of being wary of them, what if you became curious and asked:

What is the sensation of this emotion in my body?

Exactly what emotion is this?

What is the message in this feeling?

What is it asking me to do?"

Emotional Literacy of the Heart

"The moment a little boy is concerned with which is a Jay and which is a Sparrow, he can no longer see the birds or hear them sing." Eric Berne

Emotional Literacy is a serious concern today. Being able to recognize, understand and effectively express emotions are a responsible part of learning life skills. Like we learn to manage relationships, work, finances, physical health and spiritual growth, human emotion is just as relevant. Understanding emotions are vital and can overwhelm to comfort us at various times in either a negative or in a positive way.

Emotional health is a critical part of everyone's well-being. Knowing our emotions are key to success in life. If we want to make a life filled with wholesome well-being, joyousness and peace - at any age it is important to know them, and to know how to manage them.

Research proves many concerns of modern society may result in people being unable to understand and appropriately express emotion. The freedom that comes from being emotionally literate is being able to own it.

The technological world has grown exponentially and moving at a speed greater than ever been seen before in human history. Emotional literacy is just as excruciatingly a vital preventive tool. And when well understood, it can solve various social ills from violence, abuse, illness, dysfunctional relationships, and societal conflicts.

Since the 1960s, a world of experts have exploded with curiosity in forming opinions to suggested disciplines and modalities around emotional intelligence.

Emotional literacy expert, Claude Steiner, PhD in his book "Emotional Literacy; Intelligence with a Heart," says if you practice the three emotional strategies discussed in his book-opening the heart, surveying the emotional landscape, and taking responsibility-you will see dramatic changes in your emotional awareness, attitude, and in particular, Steiner states you will learn:

How to know what you want and what you feel; how to be truthful about your emotions; how to pursue fulfillment of your emotional needs.

How to manage your emotions creatively; when to hold back and when to express your feelings.

How to deal with emotional numbness or turmoil.

How to apply your knowledge of emotions at work, at home, in school, in social groups, and "on the street" to improve and deepen your relationships and forge long-lasting, honest connections with people.

How to practice a love-centered approach to personal power in a society that is moving in the direction of mistrust, loneliness, anxiety, and depression.

We've come a long way from IQ being the only standard form for determining human excellence!

Steiner professes he is not an intellectual expert. And, he shares how Research leads us into the wrong direction to prove happiness doesn't just come from having a high IQ. For example, what he says is if we have a high IQ (intelligence quotient), it's more likely we will do well in school and become productive, successful, and a good learner. Not only that, he claims, with a high IQ, we are told we'll probably have a long life and good health.

In spite of the resistance shown in some of the world's largest corporations, employers continue to battle it out to hire people with the highest IQ. However, Emotional Intelligence is ringing louder and louder at the boardroom tables forcing an arena of intelligentsia to listen up!

Emotional Intelligence, such as optimism, working with others, and empathy or compassion, are on the top 10 for 'will hire,' by employers today.

For the inquiring intellects, you'll discover Emotional Intelligence borrows from other areas of behavioural, emotional and communications theories from Albert Ellis to Alfred Adler.

Steiner's mentor is Eric Berne, Canadian-born psychiatrist known as creator of Transactional Analysis, and author of Games People Play. Berne brought us the concept of ego states to explain how humans are and how we relate to others and ways we think, feel and behave - derived from our states: "PAC: parent, adult, and child."

Steiner welcomes Daniel Goleman and his insight on Emotional Intelligence to prove having emotional awareness is as key to success as a high IQ. Not only that, he shows that you need emotional intelligence to live a "good life"-one that allows you to enjoy the riches of the spirit. To live well, he says, you need not only a high IQ but a high EQ (emotional quotient).

Some of us were taught as a child that talking about feelings or emotions were a sign of weakness. What are you feeling and what does that mean? We learn to turn feelings off, and why? "Buck up, boys and girls don't cry, toughen up - ah stop being a sissy." Do any of these remind you of what is whirling around in your head?

We cannot have EQ or Emotional literacy if we don't know how we feel, think and behave - our thoughts will drive our actions and our behaviours. Good emotional health is being aware of emotions, thoughts, feelings and behaviors, all part of working at keeping levels of stress in check. (APA).

Take this EMOTIONAL AWARENESS QUIZ:

Please answer the questions either yes or no truthfully.

1. Do you do any of these in excess e.g. drink, gamble, smoke, exercise, eat, have sex or engage in recreational drugs? - Yes or No?

2. Do you isolate yourself or feel like you do not belong or disconnected from others? - Yes or No?

3. Do you feel sad all of the time and don't know why? - Yes or No?

4. Do you get easily angry, impatient, intolerant or find yourself bullying others? - Yes or No?

5. Do find yourself catching up on years of crying over a loss - any loss? - Yes or No?

6. Do you walk around unaware of how to get beyond what the emotions inside of you are telling you? - Yes or No?

7. Do you think it is better to suppress, hold back emotions because it shows as a sign of weakness? - Yes or No?

8. Do you know how to name your emotions to help you better manage and control them? - Yes or No?

9. Do you know too little about your emotions, as something is bothering you yet don't know what to do? Yes or No?

10. Do you act happy all of the time when you are anxious, scared, lonely, discouraged? - Yes or No?

RESULTS: If you answer yes to 3 or more of these questions and no to all of the others, it is likely you are unaware of emotions. These emotions that are not brought forth from the inside out likely hold you back. Withheld emotions can impede health, and can hinder you from receiving the fulfillment you need to reach your goals and enjoy life to its utmost.

Leading by Managing Emotions

Emotions are a feedback mechanism. The dictionary defines feedback as 'information returned to the source." Thus, emotions contain information for us. They are meant to help us manage our attention. If you do not manage your emotions and pay attention to the emotions of those around you, you will miss an enormous amount of information necessary for effective leadership.

Emotional intelligence (EI) is "the ability to carry out accurate reasoning about emotions and the ability to use the emotions and emotional knowledge to enhance thought." In their extensive review of EI research, Professor John Mayer and his colleagues reported that high EI scores predict better social relations, decision-making, negotiation results, and long-term leadership success. There are four major emotional skills outlined by Professor Mayer:

1. Perceive the emotions
2. Use the emotions
3. Understand the emotional future
4. Manage the emotions

Leaders who are strong in this skill have good emotional self-control, think clearly even when they are experiencing strong emotions, and make decisions using both their heart and their head. This does not mean they don't have passionate feelings. On the contrary, they are passionate. However, they understand that a man in passion sometimes rides a mad horse. They temper their passion with reason. Here are a few strategies to help you do the same:

Stay open to emotions. Because emotions contain information, closing ourselves off to certain emotions decreases essential feedback. We seldom shut out positive emotions. Yet, ALL emotions contain information. If you find yourself shutting down when uncomfortable situations arise, try a technique psychologists call systematic desensitization:

1. Determine which emotion you would like to work on.
2. Create a list of the various situations that tend to cause that emotion.
3. List the situations from the least to the most emotionally intense.
4. D. Use your imagination to relax (e.g., progressive muscle relaxation, calm scene)
5. Generate a calm and pleasant mood.
6. Picture the least intense emotional situation.

When you find yourself becoming tense, go back to the relaxing step (D) and then generate a calm mood (E).
The goal is to visualize the emotional scene and stay open to the emotion. You begin with the easiest scenes and move slowly toward the more difficult ones.

Change your emotion. Do you ever wish you could change your emotion in a split second? If you're like me, and I know I am, that would be a great trick. Here's the real trick, you already do this. Haven't you been upset and then you've gotten a phone call, which of course you answered pleasantly? You already do this. Perhaps not consciously, but you do it. If you want to do it consistently and well, use a variation of the systematic desensitization process:

1. Determine which emotion you would like to change.
2. Select a situation that causes this emotion.

3. Use your imagination to picture that situation.

4. Bring the emotion that you want to change into a situation you have imagined.

5. Think of an interruption that could occur in that situation, such as a phone call, knock on the door, instant message, someone calling your name.

Reason with emotion. Sometimes emotions overwhelm us because we generalize them. This is what pessimistic thinkers do. They extend the negative emotion into broad areas of their lives. This is the quintessential "bring the office home" individual. I knew one executive who allowed anger at work to pervade all areas of his life. We all generalize emotions occasionally. Here's one strategy to handle it:

1. Determine which emotion you tend to exaggerate.

2. Think of a recent situation in which this emotion was present.

Answer these questions or use Morning Pages to help address them:

- Was it reasonable to feel this way?
- Do you often feel this way?
- Why do you feel this way?
- Would others interpret this situation the same way?
- Could someone interpret events differently?
- How could you think of this situation and the emotion differently?
- How might you adapt the techniques described above to help you deal with this generalization.

These strategies can help you be a better leader by managing emotions. Adapt them to your situations and style. Let me know how it goes.

Emotional Honesty: What Is Emotional Honesty?

Emotions are part of being human and this means that they play a vital role in our lives. This could be to inform one of what is going on in their immediate environment or it could have to do with something that is being triggered from their past for example.

However, no matter what their reasons for appearing are, they are trying to communicate something. And yet this form of communication doesn't always occur.

When this happens they can be repressed and ignored. If they are repressed, this can lead to all kinds of problems. And if they are not repressed, then they can be acted out, in the form of reactive and unconscious behaviour.

Emotional Honesty

To be emotionally honest, means to acknowledge and admit ones emotions. In order for one to do this, there has to be an emotional awareness in the first place. Because without an awareness of them, it will only be possible for them to be acted out or acted in.

And there will be times when it is appropriate to express ones emotions and times when it is not appropriate. What is important is that one can admit to oneself what emotions they are experiencing.

The Observer

As one is the observer of their emotions and not the emotions themselves, it means that one has the ability to be aware of each emotion. And from here, one has the choice of acting on the emotion or whether to just acknowledge the emotion.

When one does not have this ability available, there will be the tendency to be at the whim of one's emotions.

Neutral

Each emotion that one has is neutral, it is neither right or wrong, or good or bad. It just is and what makes an emotion into either of these things, is the value judgement that one labels them with.

The ego mind will categorise emotions in this way and this is due to the minds way of seeing everything in polarities. There is no middle ground to the ego mind; there are only extremes.

Identification

From here the ego mind can come to identify with certain emotions. And through this process each emotion will be classed as good or bad and right or wrong. Some emotions will be acceptable and others won't be.

The emotions that are labelled as being acceptable will end up being associated as what is safe. From here one will begin to decide what emotions they can express and what emotions they can't.

Repression

If one's ego mind has come to associate an emotion as bad or dangerous, it is likely that this emotion will then be repressed. As this happens one can end up becoming enslaved to this emotion, which is a natural result of an emotion building up.

Reactive behaviour will then occur and what should be about a two on the emotional reaction scale could end up being an eight or a nine for instance.

One's mood and emotional health will also be severely affected. Through the expression of certain emotions being denied, it will also mean that one's whole emotional spectrum will be potentially numbed and limited.

Reaction

Although one may be caught up in the repression of certain emotions, one can also end up going the other way. And this means that they feel as though they have no control over their emotions. As a result of this, one may end up constantly reacting and expressing certain emotions.

The Emotional Trap

To repress an emotion or to react to an emotion without awareness is to be enslaved to the emotion. The emotion needs to be heard and expressed from a place of awareness.

The longer the emotion is repressed or acted on, the longer it will take control. And one will have no choice other than to continually deceive not only others about what is going on, but also oneself.

Emotional Disconnection

For one to either repress or act on their emotions without awareness, it shows that one doesn't have a good connection or relationship with their emotions. And out of this emotional disharmony, all kinds of conflicts and dysfunctions are created.

This then leads to one not being able to be honest about their emotions. For if they were, these emotional difficulties wouldn't exist in the first place.

The Emotional Relationship

The relationship that one has with their emotions is usually created in the beginning of one's life. It is during this time that one's ego mind will come to associate what emotions are safe to have and what are not.

How ones caregivers respond to ones emotions will go a long way in defining whether one is comfortable with their emotions or whether they feel uncomfortable by having them. And all ones caregivers can do, is pass on the same understanding that they have with their emotions.

If they are alienated from their emotions, then they will most likely cause their child to form the same relationship with their emotions.

Early Experiences

This may have resulted from the caregivers passing on the same form of repression that they themselves had. And emotions that their ego mind had associated as unsafe become what one now sees as unsafe. The same would apply with emotions that were displayed as safe and appropriate.

And what could have been used to control the Child's emotional expression would have been the withdrawal of love and therefore ones survival would have been at risk. This could have been through: rejection, abandonment, punishment or isolation.

Emotional Acceptance

One might find that the relationship they have with their emotions, is nothing more than a reflection of the relationship that their caregivers had with their emotions. And out of being in the same environment; one ended up seeing them in the same way.

The very act of judging them as good or bad and repressing them, or getting caught up in them; is ultimately what causes the identification and attachment to them. And with this, one loses the ability to observe their emotions and to decide whether to act on them, express them to another person or to simply acknowledge there presence.

Emotional Expression

As one comes to express their emotions, either to themselves or with the help of a therapist or healer, one will begin to gain a better emotional understanding. And with this, ones emotions will begin to settle and lessen in their intensity. Through this process, repression and reactive behaviour will start to diminish.

And most importantly; one will be able to be honest to oneself about what is really going on at an emotional level.

Emotions: Do Emotions Have A Purpose?

In recent years there has been increased awareness around emotions. Before all of this came about, IQ (Intelligence quotient) was seen as the most important factor in deciding how intelligent someone is and how their life would play out.

This was until EQ (Emotional Intelligence Quotient) was introduced. Here, one's level of happiness and ability to function for example is largely associated with their level of emotional intelligence.

Emotions

For so long emotions have been portrayed as the enemies to our wellbeing and as occurrences that need to be controlled, manipulated and removed. And because of this paradigm there has been the tendency for emotions to either be repressed, suppressed or for them to be acted on.

Here one can either feel numb and completely cut off from their emotions or one can feel completely overwhelmed and constantly at the whim of their emotions. Either one of these options makes it extremely difficult for one to have emotional intelligence.

Consequences

Whether one chooses to suppress or act upon their emotions does not necessarily lead to dysfunctional consequences. Just like how eating something unhealthy once in a while is unlikely to lead to bad health.

What will lead to dysfunctional consequence is when emotions are repeatedly inhibited or are expressed and acted upon without awareness.

How Does This Look?

This can be seen externally in different kinds of addictions and compulsions. Or it can just as easily be directed inwards; with the same emotional patterns constantly appearing.

It is often said that when one's emotions are directed outward one becomes angry and when these emotions are kept inside one becomes depressed. Although that is just one example of emotional expression, what is shows is that is does not matter whether emotions are suppressed or acted out; there is still the potential for problems to occur.

Some of the common ways in which emotions are dealt with is through the consumption of alcohol, drugs and food. What these do is allow ones emotional state to be momentarily and artificial changed.

Here, the painful emotions will be suppressed and this will allow for emotions to appear that will be the complete opposite of what one was originally feeling.

Emotional Regulation

What we can see in the above example is that these external sources are being used to regulate one's emotions. The problem with using these substances is that there effects don't last and that they will inevitably lead to long term health problems if they are consistently used.

And while these substances or any other thing that changes ones emotional state are being used, all that is happening to ones emotions is that they are being avoided.

The Garden

Here I am reminded of a garden and what happens to a garden that is not looked after. One of the common problems here is that it is going to become out of control and what is likely to grow here is not flowers or fruit (Harmony), but weeds (Disharmony).

And these weeds will continue to grow and cover the whole garden, for as long as it is not cared for and nourished.

What Does This Mean?

So what has this got to do with emotions? What this shows is that the longer one runs away and denies their emotions the stronger and more powerful they will become. And as this happens, it will mean one will need more of the substances and other things to keep them at bay.

Until the day when one becomes completely numb and void of all emotional expression. Not only will one no longer feel pain any longer, but feeling all the emotions on the other side of the coin will also come to an end as well.

Why Is This?

Having emotional problems and perceiving them as troublesome may appear to be normal and how life is. But this conclusion didn't just happen and has its roots somewhere. And these roots are usually firmly rooted in one's childhood.

It is here that one typically forms their relationship with their emotions and this is a relationship that can last for a life time. And whether one sees emotions as friends or enemies will be defined during this time.

Childhood

The reason that one's childhood is so important in forming one's relationship and understanding of their emotions is because it is here that one is first exposed to emotional experiences.

At such a young age a child has no understanding of them and therefore has no way of regulating these internal processes; this causes the child to look to its caregivers.

Healthy Regulation

And how successful the child will be in this action will depend on how emotionally intelligent the caregivers are. If the caregivers themselves are in tune with their own emotions they will be able to validate, mirror and sooth the child and as this happens the child will begin to feel at ease when emotions arise.

The child will then begin to internalise this ability and as time goes it will begin to regulate its own emotions. And from the experiences of being regulated by its caregivers, it will have learnt that no matter what emotions appear it can handle them.

Nonexistent Regulation

However, if the Childs caregivers have no understanding of their own emotions then the child is going to have a completely different experience. This is probably because their caregivers were the same and out of being unaware ended up repeating the same patterns.

Here there is unlikely to be adequate external regulation for the child. An even if the child is regulated by its caregivers it will be irregular and unreliable.

The child will then have no way of dealing with these internal processes; all the child can do is sit with them. And at such a young age this will overpower the child and cause great pain and suffering.

Emotional Baggage

So not only will these children grow up with the inability to regulate their own emotions in the present moment, but they will also have years of unprocessed emotions waiting to be faced.

And if one wasn't regulated as a child, it is not a surprise that they will have emotional problems as an adult. That is not to say that one is a victim of the past. What this does is create awareness and out of awareness one has the ability to change.

Emotional Intelligence

When one was a child; emotions appeared for a reason and that reason was often due to one being in some kind of pain. And the emotions that one experiences today are no different. Ones childhood may have been many years ago, but unless that original pain has been faced and processed it will continue to appear.

These emotions may be classed as negative or positive, but they are often letting one know about what has not been looked at and what remains frozen in the body and mind.

Self Regulation

Although one might have not been regulated by their caregivers, it doesn't mean that this ability is lost forever. One can begin to regulate their emotions through self awareness.

CPSIA information can be obtained
at www.ICGtesting.com
Printed in the USA
LVHW080506200621
690690LV00013B/2075